WOMEN

DECISION MAKERS

WOMEN'S STORIES AND STRATEGIES
IN DECISION-MAKING

I0460770

BY 7 INSPIRATIONAL WOMEN AUTHORS

ISBN: 978-1-964619-90-3

TABLE OF CONTENTS

INTRODUCTION 5

The Power of a Woman Decision-Maker
By Hanna Olivas 7

Pioneering Paths and Purposeful Choices
By Adriana Luna Carlos 19

Trust, Believe, and Own Who You Are
By Jacqueline Long 26

Powerful Decisions
By Tania Vasallo 38

The Power of Style: Fashion's Influence on Women Decision-Makers
By Nermin Fathy 52

Using Your Go Power for Decision-Making
By Megan Waite 73

Celebrate Contrast – Using Conflict for Positive Transformation
By Megan Henry 93

INTRODUCTION

In ***Women Decision Makers: Women's Stories and Strategies in Decision-Making***, we celebrate the trailblazing women whose influence is reshaping the world, one decision at a time. This book dives deep into the realms where women have emerged as key players, from corporate boardrooms to political policy tables, and beyond. It illuminates the unique perspectives they bring to decision-making processes, highlighting how their leadership is not only transforming industries and institutions but also driving social change.

Through inspiring stories and firsthand accounts, *Women Decision Makers* explores the strategies these women use to navigate challenges, break barriers, and forge pathways for others to follow. Whether it's in business, government, or other critical sectors, the women featured in this book demonstrate the power of inclusive decision-making, showing how diverse perspectives lead to better outcomes for all.

As you turn the pages, you'll discover how these women have redefined leadership, using their voices and experiences to make impactful choices that resonate far beyond their roles. Their stories are a testament to the strength, resilience, and innovation that women bring to decision-making, and they stand as an inspiration for future generations of leaders. This book is not just a celebration of women's achievements—it's a call to recognize and elevate the importance of women in shaping the decisions that will define our collective future.

Hanna Olivas

Founder and CEO of SHE RISES STUDIOS

https://www.linkedin.com/company/she-rises-studios/
https://www.facebook.com/sherisesstudios
https://www.instagram.com/sherisesstudios_llc/
www.SheRisesStudios.com

Author, Speaker, and Founder. Hanna was born and raised in Las Vegas, Nevada, and has paved her way to becoming one of the most influential women of 2022. Hanna is the co-founder of She Rises Studios and the founder of the Brave & Beautiful Blood Cancer Foundation. Her journey started in 2017 when she was first diagnosed with Multiple Myeloma, an incurable blood cancer. Now more than ever, her focus is to empower other women to become leaders because The Future is Female. She is currently traveling and speaking publicly to women to educate them on entrepreneurship, leadership, and owning the female power within.

The Power of a Woman Decision-Maker

By Hanna Olivas

Being a woman decision-maker in business and life is an empowering journey that often feels daunting yet exhilarating. It's about harnessing the courage to choose, to lead, and to stand firmly in your convictions, even when the path is not clear. The power behind decision-making lies not just in the outcome of the choice but in the transformative process of self-discovery, growth, and resilience. Each decision, whether monumental or minute, shapes our destiny and carves our identity in this world.

As women, we often find ourselves at a crossroads of various responsibilities—balancing careers, families, and personal aspirations. This balancing act can lead to paralysis when faced with decisions, fueled by the fear of failure or the pressure to conform to societal expectations. I've often asked myself, "What does it truly mean to be a decision-maker?"

The Essence of Decision-Making

In my journey, I have come to understand that being a decision-maker is not merely about making choices; it is about owning the power that comes with those choices. It is about being bold enough to face uncertainty and courageous enough to embrace the consequences, both good and bad.

Let me share a story that illustrates this truth. A few years ago, I was at a pivotal moment in my career. I had the opportunity to take a position that seemed like a dream come true—a chance to lead a major project that could elevate my professional standing. However, the decision came with significant risks. It required leaving my comfort zone and stepping into uncharted territory. As I sat in my office, contemplating this leap, I felt the weight of the world on my shoulders.

The fear of failure loomed large, whispering doubts into my mind. "What if you can't handle it?" "What if you fail and lose everything you've worked for?" Yet, deep down, I knew that the opportunity to grow was greater than the fear of falling.

I took a deep breath and decided to trust myself. I accepted the position. The journey was not easy. There were moments of doubt, sleepless nights, and challenges that tested my resolve. Yet, with each hurdle, I learned to pivot, adapt, and persevere. I surrounded myself with a supportive network of women who encouraged and uplifted me, reminding me that it was okay to stumble.

Reflecting on this experience, I realized that decision-making is a skill that can be honed. It begins with understanding our values and priorities. When we are clear about what matters most to us, decision-making becomes less daunting. For example, during my journey, I learned to ask myself questions that guided my decisions: "Does this align with my values?" "Will it bring me closer to my goals?" "Am I doing this for myself or to meet someone else's expectations?"

Embracing Mistakes as Growth Opportunities

It is crucial to remember that making wrong decisions is part of the process. Each misstep is a stepping stone toward growth. I've faced decisions that led to unforeseen challenges. One such decision involved a partnership that seemed promising on paper but turned out to be misaligned with my vision. It was a tough pill to swallow. I had invested time and resources into this partnership, only to realize it was not the right fit.

In those moments of disappointment, I learned to practice self-compassion. I reminded myself that every decision carries the potential for learning. I took the time to reflect on what went wrong, adjusted my approach, and emerged stronger. The beauty of being a woman decision-maker is that we have the power to redefine our narratives, to transform our setbacks into setups for future successes.

Another powerful lesson I've learned is the importance of intuition in decision-making. As women, we often underestimate the value of our gut feelings. There have been instances where I felt compelled to make a choice that didn't necessarily make sense on paper but felt right in my heart. One particular decision stands out—a decision to pursue a passion project that had been on my mind for years.

Despite the fear of the unknown, I decided to go for it. I allocated time and resources to nurture this project, and what started as a whisper of an idea blossomed into a thriving initiative that brought joy and fulfillment into my life. This experience reinforced the idea that our intuition is a powerful guide. Listening to our inner voice can lead us to unexpected yet rewarding paths.

The Power of Collaboration

Moreover, collaboration is essential in the realm of decision-making. We often feel the pressure to have all the answers and make decisions in isolation. However, inviting others into the conversation can yield invaluable perspectives. I've learned that surrounding myself with a diverse group of individuals can enhance my decision-making process. It fosters creativity and encourages out-of-the-box thinking.

When I faced a critical decision regarding my business direction, I organized a brainstorming session with a group of trusted advisors and colleagues. Their insights illuminated aspects I had overlooked, allowing me to make a more informed choice. This collaborative approach not only enriched the decision but also fostered a sense of community and support.

The Importance of Reflection

Now, let's talk about the power of reflection in the decision-making process. After each significant decision, I've made it a practice to reflect on the outcome—what worked, what didn't, and what I learned. This practice allows me to grow and evolve continuously. It also instills confidence in my ability to navigate future choices.

Life is a series of decisions, and each decision is an opportunity for growth. The act of deciding can be liberating, and as women, we hold the keys to unlocking our potential. Embracing the power of decision-making means stepping into our authenticity and recognizing that we have the strength to forge our paths.

Our Shared Journey

As I navigate the intricate landscape of decision-making, I am reminded of the strength we share as women. Our journeys may differ, but the challenges we face and the victories we celebrate are interconnected. Every time we choose to uplift one another, we create a ripple effect that can inspire countless others.

Let me take you back to a moment that reinforced this sense of community. A few years ago, I attended a women's leadership conference. The room was filled with remarkable women from diverse backgrounds, each sharing their stories of triumph and struggle. I remember one particular session where a panel of accomplished women spoke candidly about their journeys, including the tough decisions they faced along the way.

Listening to them, I realized that the fear and doubt I had felt in my decision-making process were universal. Their stories resonated with my own experiences, reminding me that I was not alone in my struggles. We exchanged ideas, offered support, and forged connections that would last long after the conference ended. This experience highlighted the importance of creating spaces where women can share their stories and learn from one another.

Celebrating Our Uniqueness

Being a woman decision-maker also means embracing our uniqueness. Each of us brings a distinct perspective to the table, shaped by our experiences, culture, and values. Our voices matter, and they deserve to be heard.

In my career, I've made it a point to amplify the voices of women who have been historically underrepresented. By creating opportunities for others to share their insights and participate in decision-making processes, we can foster a culture of inclusivity and empowerment. When we lift each other up, we not only enrich our own lives but also contribute to the greater good of society.

The Unseen Challenges

Yet, the path of decision-making is not without its unseen challenges. It's easy to portray decision-making as a straightforward process, but the reality is that it is often fraught with emotional and psychological hurdles. Each decision carries the weight of our past experiences, insecurities, and fears, and it can feel overwhelming at times.

I remember a time when I had to decide whether to leave a toxic work environment. On the surface, it seemed like an easy choice. Who would want to stay in a place that drained their energy and stifled their growth? Yet, the fear of the unknown kept me tethered. What if I left and couldn't find another job? What if I regretted my decision? The "what-ifs" flooded my mind, making it challenging to see the light beyond the darkness.

Eventually, I realized that I was holding myself back. I was allowing fear to dictate my decisions. After much contemplation, I made the leap and left that job. The relief and freedom I felt were overwhelming. It was a reminder that sometimes, the hardest decisions lead to the most significant breakthroughs.

Nurturing Self-Trust

One of the most profound aspects of decision-making is cultivating self-trust. It's about believing in your abilities and intuition, even when doubt creeps in. I've learned to embrace the mantra, "Trust the process." This mindset encourages me to view decision-making as a journey rather than a destination.

Every decision I make, right or wrong, contributes to my growth. It is through the act of deciding that I discover my strengths and weaknesses. This process has taught me to view setbacks as opportunities for growth. Each misstep has become a stepping stone toward a more profound understanding of myself and what I truly want.

As women, we have the unique opportunity to support one another in this journey. Sharing our experiences, whether they involve triumphs or tribulations, helps to create a culture of understanding and encouragement. I have often found solace in conversations with other women who have navigated similar paths. We talk openly about our fears, dreams, and the decisions that have shaped our lives.

I remember a coffee meeting with a dear friend who had just made a significant career change. As she recounted her story, I could see the determination in her eyes. Yet, beneath that strength lay a vulnerability that we both shared. We laughed about the moments of doubt, the late-night anxiety, and the sheer audacity it takes to pursue a new path. By the end of our conversation, I felt more empowered, knowing that we were in this together, navigating the complexities of decision-making side by side.

This sense of sisterhood is crucial. When we create safe spaces for women to share their stories, we validate each other's experiences. We remind one another that it's okay to feel uncertain. In these moments, we learn to embrace the messiness of decision-making and appreciate the beauty of growth that comes from it.

The Courage to Lead

As I reflect on my journey, I recognize that being a decision-maker is also about having the courage to lead. Leadership is not just about occupying a position of power; it is about being a beacon of hope for others. As women, we possess unique qualities—empathy, intuition, resilience—that make us natural leaders.

When I stepped into a leadership role, I realized that my decisions could impact not just my life but the lives of those around me. I learned to approach leadership with a sense of responsibility and purpose. Each choice I made was an opportunity to inspire others, to create a culture of inclusivity, and to encourage my team to thrive.

One particular moment stands out when I had to make a decision that would affect my entire team. We were at a crossroads, facing a challenging project that required a shift in strategy. As the leader, I had to rally my team, communicate openly about our options, and involve everyone in the decision-making process. It was a delicate balance between guiding the team and empowering them to voice their opinions.

We held a series of brainstorming sessions, where every team member contributed their thoughts. It was during these discussions that I realized the true power of collaboration. The diverse perspectives enriched our decision-making process, leading us to a solution that everyone felt invested in. When we finally executed our plan, the sense of accomplishment we shared was palpable. It reminded me that leadership is about lifting others and creating an environment where everyone feels valued.

The Ripple Effect of Decisions

Every decision we make creates a ripple effect, not just in our lives but in the lives of those around us. The choices we make have the power to inspire change and foster growth. I often think about the legacy of my decisions—how they contribute to the larger narrative of empowerment for women.

A poignant example of this was when I made a conscious decision to mentor young women in my community. I wanted to give back, to help others navigate the challenges I had faced. By sharing my experiences, offering guidance, and creating opportunities, I realized that I could contribute to a collective movement of empowered women.

During one of our mentorship sessions, a young woman shared her dream of starting her own business. Her passion was infectious, but she hesitated due to self-doubt. I recalled my own journey, filled with uncertainty and fear, but I encouraged her to take the leap. I shared my own stories of missteps and triumphs, and as she listened, I could see her confidence begin to blossom.

That moment was transformative—for both of us. I realized that by empowering her to make decisions about her future, I was also affirming my own journey. The ripple effect of decision-making became evident; when we empower one another, we create a tidal wave of strength that can reshape our communities.

Navigating Life's Complexities

Life is inherently complex, and the decisions we face are often layered with challenges. There are moments when external factors—societal expectations, family responsibilities, financial constraints—make it difficult to choose a path. Yet, it is precisely in these moments that our strength shines through.

I recall a particularly challenging period when I had to balance my responsibilities as a mother, business leader, and community advocate. The pressure was overwhelming, and I found myself at a crossroads. I had the opportunity to take on a significant role in a community project, but it would require considerable time and energy. As I weighed my options, I felt torn between my desire to contribute and the fear of neglecting my family.

After much contemplation, I decided to engage my family in the decision-making process. I shared my aspirations with them and sought their input. To my surprise, they encouraged me to pursue the opportunity, expressing their support and excitement for the project. This experience taught me that decision-making is not always a solitary endeavor; involving those we love can lead to powerful insights and support.

The Power of Resilience

Resilience is a crucial trait for any woman decision-maker. Life will undoubtedly throw obstacles our way, but how we respond to those challenges defines our journeys. When I faced setbacks, I learned to embrace resilience as a guiding principle.

One particularly trying moment occurred when I encountered financial difficulties in my business. It felt like the ground was crumbling beneath me, and uncertainty loomed large. In those moments, I had to dig deep and find the strength to make tough decisions about the future of my business.

Rather than succumbing to despair, I chose to view the situation as an opportunity for growth. I sought advice from mentors, reassessed my business strategies, and explored innovative solutions. It was a grueling process, but each decision brought me closer to clarity.

Through resilience, I learned that setbacks do not define us; rather, they serve as catalysts for transformation. My ability to adapt and pivot in the face of adversity became a testament to my strength as a woman decision-maker.

Conclusion: The Journey of Empowerment

In conclusion, being a woman decision-maker in business and life is an empowering journey filled with lessons, growth, and community. It is about embracing our power to choose, supporting one another, and navigating the complexities of life with resilience and courage.

As we reflect on our experiences, let us celebrate the uniqueness we each bring to the decision-making process. Together, we can create a ripple effect of empowerment that transcends our individual journeys. Our decisions shape not only our lives but the lives of those around us.

As women, we hold the keys to unlocking our potential and making a profound impact on the world. Let us embrace the journey, cherish our experiences, and continue to uplift one another as we forge ahead.

Conclusion: The Journey Continues

In conclusion, being a woman decision-maker in business and life is a journey filled with empowerment, growth, and resilience. It is about embracing our power to choose, learn from our experiences, and uplift one another along the way. Let us celebrate our unique journeys, cherish our decision-making abilities, and remember that every choice we make is a testament to our strength. Together, we can illuminate the world with our collective wisdom and create a brighter future for ourselves and generations to come.

Adriana Luna Carlos

Founder and CEO of SHE RISES STUDIOS & FENIX TV

https://www.linkedin.com/in/adriana-luna-carlos/
https://www.facebook.com/adrianalunacarlos
https://www.instagram.com/sherisesstudios_llc/
https://www.sherisesstudios.com/
https://fenixtv.app/

Adriana Luna Carlos is an accomplished web and graphic designer, author, and mentor with a passion for helping women succeed in life and business. With over 10 years of experience in graphic and web arts, Adriana has built a reputation as an innovative leader and entrepreneur. In 2020, she co-founded She Rises Studios, a multi-digital media company and publishing house that has helped countless clients achieve their branding and marketing goals. In 2023, she co-created FENIX TV, an online streaming platform that showcases stories of people breaking barriers, shattering stereotypes, and triumphing against the odds.

As an advocate for women's success, Adriana challenges her clients and mentees to strive for nothing less than excellence. She has a deep understanding of the insecurities and challenges that women often face in the business world and provides the guidance and resources needed to overcome them. Her success as a business leader and entrepreneur has made her a sought-after mentor and speaker at events around the world.

Through her work, Adriana has demonstrated a commitment to creating opportunities for women to succeed in business and life. Her passion for innovation, leadership, and women's empowerment has made her a respected figure in the business community, and her impact will undoubtedly continue to inspire and empower women for years to come.

Pioneering Paths and Purposeful Choices

By Adriana Luna Carlos

Decision-making is more than just a task; it's a responsibility, a privilege, and often, a challenge. As women, the choices we make ripple far beyond ourselves, influencing our families, communities, and the professional spaces we occupy. My journey in decision-making hasn't been without its struggles, but every choice I've made has shaped me into the leader I am today.

Growing up in a family that deeply valued hard work and integrity, I learned early on that decisions weren't just about outcomes—they were about aligning your actions with your values. "We say what we mean, and we do what we say," my family would often remind me. This principle has been my compass in both my personal and professional life, guiding me to navigate uncertainty, take bold risks, and lead with authenticity.

The Weight of Choices

For many of us, decision-making isn't just a skill; it's a daily practice. From the moment we wake up, we're faced with a myriad of choices. Some are small and seemingly inconsequential, while others have the power to alter the trajectory of our lives and the lives of those around us. As I reflect on my own experiences, I realize that the hardest decisions are often the ones that challenge us to step outside our comfort zones, confront our fears, and trust our instincts.

One of the most pivotal moments in my life came when I co-founded She Rises Studios. The decision to step into a leadership role during uncertain times, amid a global pandemic, was not one I took lightly. I knew that creating a platform for empowering women meant making sacrifices and embracing challenges head-on. It meant being prepared to make decisions that weren't always popular but were necessary for the vision I believed in.

Navigating Challenges with Clarity

Women often face unique challenges in decision-making roles, particularly in male-dominated spaces. There's an unspoken pressure to prove ourselves, to justify our choices, and to constantly deliver results. Early in my career, I found myself second-guessing decisions, not because I lacked confidence in my abilities but because I feared judgment. I worried about being seen as "too bold" or "too emotional."

But over time, I realized that the fear of making a wrong decision was holding me back more than any potential mistake ever could. I learned to trust my instincts and lean into the values that had been instilled in me. When faced with uncertainty, I asked myself, "What is the best choice for the greater good? What aligns most with my purpose?" Answering these questions helped me find clarity and move forward with confidence.

One particular example stands out. A few years ago, I was faced with a tough decision about whether to take a financial risk in expanding our initiatives at She Rises Studios. The opportunity was exciting but came with significant uncertainties. After careful consideration, I chose to move forward, not because I was sure it would succeed, but because I believed in the impact it could have. That decision taught me that even in the face of risk, leading with purpose and vision can create incredible opportunities.

The Emotional Side of Decision-Making

It's impossible to talk about decision-making without addressing the emotional weight it carries. As women, we often balance logic with empathy, ensuring that our choices consider not just data and outcomes but also the people they affect. While this balance can be a strength, it can also make decisions feel heavier.

For me, this has been especially true in personal decisions. Choosing to prioritize my health over my work, or deciding to step back and rest when everything inside me wanted to push forward, were moments when I had to confront my own limits. These choices weren't easy, but they were necessary. They reminded me that good decision-making isn't about being invincible—it's about being honest with yourself and making choices that serve your long-term well-being.

One of the most emotionally charged decisions I've ever made was when I chose to speak out about my personal struggles, including my experiences with health and infertility. Sharing something so personal felt vulnerable, but it was a decision rooted in my desire to connect with and inspire others. That choice taught me the power of authenticity and the importance of making decisions that align with your truth.

Strategies for Strong Decision-Making

Over the years, I've developed strategies that have helped me navigate the complexities of decision-making. These strategies aren't about making the "perfect" choice but about making thoughtful, intentional ones:

1. **Define Your Core Values:** Knowing what matters most to you—whether it's integrity, compassion, or growth—provides a foundation for your decisions. When faced with tough choices, I often ask myself, "Does this align with my values?"

2. **Gather Diverse Perspectives:** While it's important to trust your instincts, seeking input from others can provide valuable insights. Surround yourself with people who challenge and inspire you, and don't be afraid to ask for advice.

3. **Embrace the Power of Pause:** In our fast-paced world, we often feel pressured to make decisions quickly. Taking a moment to pause, reflect, and gather your thoughts can lead to more deliberate and effective choices.

4. **Learn from Every Outcome:** Not every decision will lead to success, and that's okay. Viewing each choice as a learning opportunity helps you grow and approach future decisions with greater wisdom.

5. **Lead with Empathy:** Whether you're making decisions in a professional or personal context, considering the impact on others fosters trust and collaboration. Empathy is a strength, not a weakness.

Celebrating Women in Leadership

As women, our presence in decision-making roles is transformative. We bring unique perspectives, lived experiences, and a deep understanding of the interconnectedness of people and processes. Our ability to balance empathy with strategy, creativity with logic, and collaboration with independence makes us invaluable leaders.

Throughout history, women have made groundbreaking decisions that have shaped the world—from activists fighting for justice to CEOs redefining industries. Yet, many of our contributions remain underrecognized. That's why books like *Women Decision Makers* are so important. They shine a light on the incredible impact women have in shaping the future.

Empowering the Next Generation

One of my greatest joys is mentoring and empowering other women to step into decision-making roles. I believe that when we lift each other up, we create a ripple effect that benefits everyone. Whether it's through sharing knowledge, offering encouragement, or simply being a role model, we have the power to inspire the next generation of women leaders.

To the women reading this, know that your voice matters. Your perspective is valuable, and your decisions have the power to create meaningful change. Whether you're leading a team, managing a household, or making choices for your own growth, you are shaping the world in ways that are uniquely yours.

A Call to Action

As we celebrate the impact of women in decision-making, let us also commit to supporting one another. Let's create spaces where women feel empowered to take risks, to speak their truth, and to lead with authenticity. Let's challenge the biases that hold us back and advocate for a future where women's voices are heard and valued in every sphere.

To every woman reading this: You are a decision-maker. Whether your choices affect a family, a company, or a community, they matter. Embrace your role with confidence, lead with purpose, and know that every decision you make brings us closer to a world where women's leadership is celebrated and normalized.

Jacqueline Long

CEO of Elevate Your Biz Digital Consulting, LLC
Business Marketing Strategist

https://www.facebook.com/groups/elevatedfemaleentrepreneur/
https://www.instagram.com/elevateyourbizllc/
http://www.elevateyourbizcoaching.com/

Jacqueline is a Business Marketing Strategist, Podcast Host, Master Certified Life, Transformation & Mindset Coach, to female entrepreneurs. She is also the Co-author of two Anthologies for women in business, Purpose Driven Paycheck and Becoming an Unstoppable Woman Entrepreneur II.

Over the last several years, Jacqueline has helped women start and scale their coaching businesses, breakthrough their limiting beliefs and master their sales and marketing strategies online. She is currently in the process of transitioning her business to specialize in book writing/coaching, digital course creation and podcast marketing in her business. Jacqueline is the founder of Elevate Your Biz Consulting, LLC - her official brand dedicated to women achieving the next level of their dreams, by building profitable online businesses.

Jacqueline holds three advanced degrees (Master of Science in Human Resources Management, Master of Public Administration & Master of

Arts in Criminal Justice). Prior to starting her coaching business 7 years ago, she had a 20+ year career in non-profit senior management. She has formerly served as a Director of Case Management, Director of Social Services, Director of Clinical Trials, and Vice President of Human resources.

Jacqueline is a native New Yorker who enjoys traveling, reading, journaling, and spending time with her large family. She has two young adult daughters, who are graduate students, and she lives in the Atlanta Metro-Area.

Currently, Jacqueline is managing her consulting business, working on her first solo book, and pursuing her PhD in Education, specializing in e-Learning for adults.

You can find Jacqueline and learn more about Elevate Your Biz Coaching & Consulting in the following places...

1. The Elevated Female Entrepreneur Community on Facebook for coaches & service providers at: www.elevatedfemales.com
2. The Elevated Female Podcasters community: https://bit.ly/ElevatedFemalePodcasters
3. Official site: www.elevateyourbizcoaching.com
4. Podcast: Women Elevating Women – Apple Podcasts.

Trust, Believe, and Own Who You Are

By Jacqueline Long

"We need to accept that we don't always make the right decisions, that we'll screw up royally sometimes. Understand that failure is not the opposite of success, it's part of success."
—Arianna Huffington, Founder & CEO, Thrive Global

The first difficult, but meaningful career decision I ever made was whether to take on the challenge of leading and managing a program that was on the verge of being canceled by the contracting source. While I had the experience, I had a lot of reservations and some self-doubt about the position because it was a program in chaos, that would require a lot of work and effort. At the time, I had young children at home and wasn't sure that I wanted to take on a stressful senior management position, once again. But I did it, and it would be one of the most challenging and rewarding decisions of my career.

In the mid-2000s, I was hired as the Director of Social Services for a case management and advocacy program for people living with HIV/AIDS. The previous director had been terminated, the program had been audited and found to be out of compliance and on the verge of cancellation, by the NYS Department of AIDS Institute, the state contracting source. It was a COBRA Case Management program (also known as a Medicaid billable advocacy and support program in New York), where the staff was assigned to work in teams of three, consisting of a case manager, case manager technician, and community follow-up worker. The objective of the case management teams was to provide support and social service advocacy for the individuals or families to adjust to being HIV positive or living with the diagnosis and additional co-existing substance use or mental health issues. This model was assigned by the state contracting agency and could not be changed.

Therefore, an essential part of the job was the ability for case management staff to work well within a three-person team setting, and client services to be rendered and billed. I had been tasked, as the new director, to make some immediate, major changes and improvements to the program that would start the program on its way to compliance, within 90 days of the audit.

So where do you start with a program in jeopardy of losing its contract? What do you do when you must correct several program problems before the next contractor audit/review within 90 days of your hire? And what do you do when you have programs systems that are non-existent and failing, with underperforming employees, and low program morale?

Decisions, decisions, decisions...

MY STORY

First, here's a little about me. I grew up in a traditional Caribbean family, of mixed African, Chinese, and European ancestry, from the twin islands of Trinidad and Tobago. I am the youngest of fourteen children and a first-generation American. I was raised in the tough community of Flatbush, Brooklyn, and learned very early in life, that the key to a brighter future was hard work, focus, and education. I had a mother who imparted to me that I could do and have anything if I believed and thought positively. I would learn throughout my life and career, that she was a thousand percent right. There was no push or demand for me to go to college, however, after graduating from high school valedictorian, it felt like the next logical step. So, not knowing what to do next, and with the support of my parents, I went to college.

After college, I worked full-time as an HIV housing case manager, and HIV Pre- & Post-test counselor, testing women for the HIV virus and counseling them on their results. I went on to earn three master's degrees. I worked hard, learned a lot, and moved up to middle and then senior management, quickly. I held several positions in the nonprofit sector in NYC: Director of Social Services, Director of Case Management, and a Vice-President of Human Resources. I enjoyed coaching, supervising, hiring, and managing people, budgets, and departments. But after 20-plus years, I felt burnt out and frustrated. I needed a challenge. You see, I did everything "right". You know, the way we were taught to traditionally—go to college, get a good job, work for many years, earn a good retirement pension, and retire.

After working my way up the career ladder, I was bored. I was tired of working long hours and spending less time with my family. I was frustrated with management politics, nepotism, and staff turnover. I was sick of projects I had no interest in and only 3% annual raises. But I was especially tired of budget restraints, management politics, and the C-suite wanting MORE, for less. At times, I absolutely hated waking up to go to work. I was done! It was time for a change. I started to think, "I want to start my own business." BUT it was so risky. I HAD to work. I had bills, student loans, and a family to support. How could I?

Walking away from my career, an excellent salary and benefits was foolish. That's what I was told repeatedly. But, after many years of managing other people's businesses, I had finally had ENOUGH! A job, even a professional one, was NO longer what I wanted. I had learned a lot, and it was time to pursue my own dream. But, whenever I talked about wanting to start my own business, I heard many discouraging things, like, "really?" "you're crazy", and "that's dumb". I even gave some of those people in my life the pink slip. You were either with me, or you had to go. It was going to be a tough and scary journey without the noise and negativity.

MORE LIFE-CHANGING DECISIONS

In 2013, I made a life-changing decision. I left my job, moved my family to Georgia, and started a new life. Two years later, I would build a profitable brand and coaching/consulting business. Fast forward, here I am now, with no regrets.

That's how it started and played out for me. I made some important and tough decisions—life-changing decisions—along the way. But it has been an amazing learning experience. I've had many successes. But it also hasn't been all peaches and cream. I struggled at times. I've had challenges and setbacks that made me question my decisions, my ability, and my sanity. I doubted myself, I invested and didn't achieve revenue goals, I had launches that failed, and I even gave up once or twice. Business and being a CEO and decision-maker was challenging. But I failed and pushed forward anyway. During it all, I was also managing my personal life. I was raising two girls, and I was injured in a car accident, requiring months of therapy to recover.

After recovering from my accident, my mother's health deteriorated, and I would care for her until she passed in early 2020. I regrouped from these setbacks and got clear on what I wanted next. I focused on my business, watched my girls graduate and move on to college, and started the long-term goal of becoming an author and pursuing my PhD in the winter of 2022.

TAKING ACTION & TRUSTING MYSELF

Now back to my initial story: a program in chaos, a new director, and a pending 90-day compliance review. I had a lot on my plate with my new position and program. I had the huge responsibility of steering a struggling program back to compliance. Oh, where to start?

During the first two weeks in the Director's position, I was terrified. The pressure was almost unbearable. But I had to set aside my fear and self-doubt and trust my experience and ability to get things done. I knew what had to be done, so the fear was just my inner negative self-talk. The first week, I had to learn and assess systems and employees in the organization and make some tough decisions quickly. I met with staff individually to learn who they were and met with management and the departments that I had to work closely with (i.e., Accounting and HR).

I assessed the systems, such as staff meetings, documentation and entering billing into the systems, team functioning, and more. And I worked closely with my new administrative assistant to learn and delegate outstanding program matters that needed to be addressed immediately. I took extensive notes and planned. I had been doing this for a long time and had extensive experience with case management programs and the HIV/AIDS population, so even though I was terrified out of my mind, I had no time to feel the fear. I had to take action and create a corrective action plan, immediately.

I had been recommended for the position by the state contractor because I knew the work and had the experience to reorganize and renew similar programs. Therefore, my extensive background would help me assess and make important decisions quickly, ultimately bringing the struggling program back to contractual compliance within 6 months of being hired.

To start, what were some of the things I did and decisions that I made, to get the program on track, you might be thinking? Well, in my first 45 days, I made decisions in 10 major areas, that started the program on its way to official state compliance. Many of my decisions were based on the contractual and specific needs of the COBRA Case Management program. Below are just a few:

1. Implemented bi-weekly staff meetings for the first three months.
2. Updated new systems for documentation submission and required review and sign-off by supervisors.
3. Implemented required weekly supervision with supervisors and their teams for discussions about documentation, client cases, and team discussions and challenges.
4. Established an annual staff training calendar and sign-ups for training, to meet the required annual 77 hours of staff HIV/AIDS and case management training.

5. Established a new orientation and five-day training for new staff, that included training by supervisors based on their case management expertise. I trained staff on

6. Assessed staff performances and succession planning—who would stay, and who needed to be placed on performance improvement plans. And yes, three staff members were terminated and replaced.

7. Reviewed the budget and deficit, to determine what cuts and improvements needed to be made to improve case management billing.

8. Implemented supervision with the supervisory staff, monthly, to discuss the support the supervisors and site directors and their teams needed from me.

9. Recruited and hired new staff, to fill vacant billable positions.

10. Established new staff policies for staff fieldwork, reporting to the office.

11. Established open-door communication, staff of the month, birthday and holiday program celebrations, and an employee suggestion box, to improve employee morale.

The first decisions I made while working to improve the program were related to staffing and policies. But the most important decision I made was to believe in myself and welcome the tough challenge of leading a failing program, while trusting my decision-making, as a woman, surrounded by male managerial counterparts. I embraced my authentic self and had the confidence to step up and meet the challenge. Six months later, the program was audited for the last time and taken off corrective action. We were even approved for an additional team, after 12 months of my leading the program.

OWN WHO YOU ARE

I shared both my career and personal experiences here to demonstrate one important thing in both life and career, the importance of decision-making, in all that we do. While we may not be conscious of it, we are making simple and tough decisions in our lives, businesses, and careers, every day, and as women, we are not always given the credit for how much and how well we do it. We sometimes do not even appreciate or trust ourselves, for the many decisions we make and juggle, to improve our lives and the lives of those we love. When it comes to professional advancement, we are often second-guessed for our abilities to make tough decisions. We are overlooked and dismissed as too emotional or not experienced or savvy enough to make sound decisions simply because we are women. It has been argued, by men usually, that women are emotional and overly sensitive, therefore, these traits make us irrational or poor decision-makers. But the truth is when used effectively, emotion can be a secret weapon and superpower in the board room. In my opinion, women leaders often make better decisions than their male counterparts. As women, we have traits such as creativity, intuition, and empathy that give us a keen sense of emotional intelligence, which is an important skill for developing relationships, managing people, and managing oneself, which results in sound decision-making in our personal and professional lives. We use these traits to develop, think, and feel things out in the decision-making process. Women are prepared and organized, not ashamed to articulate what they don't understand, think diversely, and bring deeper and richer discussions and problem-solving ideas to the table when they are in decision-making roles (Wiersema and Mors, 2023). Women are just as capable, if not in some cases, more prepared to take on the challenge of top decision-makers as leaders and entrepreneurs.

The most important thing we, as women, need to learn to be effective decision-makers is owning our femininity, and mastering the art of authentic decision-making, by using our instincts, skills, and emotions as the powerful tools that they are, in making the best decisions in any situation. No shade to Steve Harvey regarding his book, *Act Like a Lady, Think Like a Man,* where he discusses how women should act and think in relationships. The truth is, however, that women do not ever have to think like a man in anything they do. We are quite capable of thinking and acting like women, being successful in careers, business, and relationships, thinking on our own, and using our own feminine traits.

While most major company and business decision-makers today are male, more women are assuming roles as leaders in decision-making positions. And the last thing we need as women is advice from men on how we "should" think or behave. I can attest to the fact that it's difficult to work amongst men. But I can also share that I personally never had to take on masculine traits to lead or make decisions effectively while earning the respect of my team. It's important that we are ourselves, as women, and we are accepted with the special skills, talents, and qualifications we have to offer. I want you to know and believe that no matter the circumstances, you can think like a woman and use all your amazing feminine qualities to be successful as a CEO, business leader, and decision-maker. Therefore, as a leader and decision-maker, start with the decision to be YOU and own every bit of your talents, skills, and womanhood. Lead and make decisions with femininity and grace.

THE SUCCESSFUL DECISION MAKER

What does it take to become a successful and authentic woman decision-maker? It takes a woman who embraces her femininity and is focused on improving herself and expanding her skills and experiences, so she has more to offer and can never be labeled as "not qualified".

Making sound decisions in life and business, to me, is not only about doing what's best but also about owning who you are and making decisions, using your inherent and learned skills. It's about disabusing ourselves of the notion that we must lead or make decisions the way men do to be successful, or that we must adopt masculine ways of thinking to be accepted. What we must do, however, is work on skills that help us to lead and make decisions in a way that is feminine and authentic to who we are as women. It's about embracing our feminine power, developing our self-awareness and leadership skills, and using them to our advantage. To be an authentic women decision-maker, develop your creativity, trust your intuition, think critically, be empathic, but firm, be vulnerable, but not a pushover, and use your emotional intelligence to manage yourself and others.

RECOMMENDATIONS FOR SUCCESS

Finally, to become a better decision-maker, develop these hard and soft professional skills for success:

1. Investigate the situation before you in detail.
2. Assess the information you have and weigh your options, or pros and cons.
3. Establish a culture that fosters and encourages input and feedback for employees and stakeholders in the decision-making process.
4. Select the best solution or decision.
5. Develop a plan with time frames.
6. Share your plan and take action.
7. Evaluate the plan and make changes and updates when possible.
8. Assess what went well and what you could do better or change for future decision-making.

Develop these skills and surround yourself with other female mentors, and like-minded women in business, to support you in the journey. Be successful, work on yourself, and do it without compromising who you are as a woman or leader. You have so much to offer.

Elevate!

References

Wiersema, M., & Mors, L. M. (2023, November 13). Research: How Women Improve Decision-Making on Boards. Harvard Business Review.
https://hbr.org/2023/11/research-how-women-improve-decision-making-on-boards

Tania Vasallo

Founder of The Courage To Be

https://www.linkedin.com/in/tania-vasallo-2aa3852a/
https://web.facebook.com/tania.vasallo.5
https://www.instagram.com/thecouragetobehappy/
https://www.thecouragetobehappy.com/
https://taniavasallo.lpages.co/the-courage-to-be-podcast/

Tania Vasallo is the host of The Courage To Be Podcast, one of the top 1.5% ranking podcasts in the world.

She is an International speaker, a Napoleon Hill certified coach, a Money Mindset and Success Expert, An Event Host, Business Mentor, Investor, Philanthropist and Mom.

Born to a Spanish father, an American mother and raised in Spain, Tania was constantly in search of freedom from a patriarchal society. She now specializes in teaching the science of the mind and transforming people's limiting beliefs so they can make more money, achieve their desired success and live a lifestyle of freedom!

Tania has helped hundreds of people to heal their money stories and a group of 22 people manifest over $1.2 million within 60 days.

Tania and her family currently make their home in Santa Fe, New Mexico. When she isn't busy helping her clients be their best selves, Tania enjoys traveling, visiting her family in Spain, exploring nature and experiencing all of the adventures life has to offer.

Powerful Decisions

By Tania Vasallo

The quality of your life is based on the quality of your decisions. Please re-read this statement.

The quality of your life is based on the quality of your decisions.

What kind of decisions are you making? Are they quality decisions or are they unimportant decisions?

How many decisions do you think we make in a day? 50? 100? 1000? Approximately 30,000 decisions a day. And 95-98% of those decisions are automatic. They are decisions that are not really quality decisions.

Let's delve into understanding what a decision is and how we can make a quality decision. The quality of a decision is not just in its impact but also in its alignment with our values and goals.

Consider the story of Napoleon Hill and Andrew Carnegie. Over a century ago, Andrew Carnegie invited Napoleon Hill to his home. Carnegie, a multimillionaire, lamented that the secrets of success were being taken to the grave by successful men. He proposed that Hill dedicate 20 years to researching the principles of success. Carnegie would open doors and introduce Hill to successful individuals, but he chose not to pay him. Hill had to decide within 60 seconds. Hill answered in 29 seconds, saying yes, a decision that changed his life and impacted millions of people through his work. This was a quality decision, made quickly and with conviction.

Successful people make decisions quickly and are slow to change them. The bigger the decision, the greater the value and confidence it brings. Decisions should not be based on current circumstances but on faith in oneself and the belief that the universe will provide.

The second characteristic that I want to comment on is that when we look at the process of decisions, the bigger and more difficult the decision, the greater the value it's going to require. But there's also an advantage: the greater is the confidence that you acquire at the end of that decision, and the universe will shower you with greater rewards.

The third characteristic of a quality decision is that you can't make decisions based on the circumstances you have now. Because the circumstances you have now are simply the results of the thoughts you had in the past.

If your bank account is at a minimum, it's because you've been having thoughts, and you've been in that space of thought where you haven't been able to generate money. So, you can't make decisions based on where you are right now. You have to make decisions without knowing how you will achieve that goal.

The problem is that we've been taught to make decisions in an incorrect way. Many of us don't make decisions unless we know HOW to get there. For example, if you're given an opportunity to take a course, and you say "but I don't have the money, how am I going to pay for it? I don't have the time, how am I going to find time? How?" You're making a decision based on your circumstances right now, instead of based on your confidence in yourself, in having faith and knowing that you can solve this problem. The how will only be revealed once you make that decision.

Think about a moment in your life when you made a decision that changed the course of your life. Think about that moment when you asked someone out, when you decided to get married, when you decided to get that job that you didn't know you were going to get, when you decided to move out of town, when you decided to start a new career...

There are two, three, four, maybe five key decisions you made in your life that changed the course of your life.

The following is a story about a decision I made years ago that changed the course of my life. And that decision was when I finished college I went to work at an advertising agency in New York City.

I was interning there for eight months, and I realized that one of the things I wanted, and desired the most was to become an Art Director.

When we have a definiteness of purpose, the decisions start to be of higher quality. If you don't have a defined purpose, I invite you to craft your definite major purpose. Once you have a major purpose then desires start showing up.

When I worked in that advertising agency, I realized that I wanted to work as an art director. I wanted to be in the creative department.

But, in order to work in the creative department, you needed to have a portfolio. And I didn't have a portfolio. So I said, well, the first thing I'm going to do is go to a school that prepares you to have a portfolio.

There weren't many schools here in the United States that offered a master's degree in art direction. There were only four schools. One in New York, one in California, one in Atlanta, and one in Miami.

Here's what happens when you make a decision, in my case "I'm going to study art direction."

The next thing that always happens when you make a decision, especially a big decision, is that fears start to appear:

- The fear of poverty
- the fear of criticism,
- the fear of losing the love of a loved one,
- the fear of illness,
- the fear of old age, and
- the fear of death.

You have to ask yourself, when you have to make a decision, the first thing that's going to come up is that fear.

The fear comes from the amygdala in the brain. Its function is to keep us safe. Thousands of years ago, it made sense for the amygdala to keep us safe when we saw a lion in the jungle.

But today, we don't see lions in the jungle. Our lions are imaginary. You have to analyze what your amygdala is doing when you're getting nervous, when those fears come in, when that anxiety creeps in.

What the amygdala of the brain is doing, the reptilian part of the brain, it's sounding all the alarms and it's giving you all the reasons and all the excuses to not make that decision that's going to bring you closer to your dersire. You have to pay attention to this, to see what's going on!

Going back to my story: I'm in New York and I start looking at these schools and I say, "where do I want to go to study? I discarded New York because I already studied in that school.

I went to Pasadena and they asked me for four years to go back to studying and I didn't want to spend the money and do that. There were two more schools left. One in Atlanta, but the same founder of the Atlanta school had founded a school in Miami that only had seven students. It wasn't a very well-known school.

I finished my internship and I went to Florida to visit my grandparents who were living there. And I asked them if they didn't mind driving me down to this school in Miami.

It was a four-hour drive. I went to the school, I did an interview, I fell in love!

That burning desire came back to me, it started to grow more and more in my heart. And I decided that I wanted to study at this school.

The problem was that it cost $30,000 for two years. I kept wondering "how am I going to pay for this school?

The fear of poverty began to arise: "where am I going to get the money from? I don't have this kind of money, maybe I shouldn't go there. This was a stupid idea anyway..." But I intuitively knew that I had to take action.

The next steps after making the decision are to confront the fear, have faith and take action.

That's where you connect with your courage. You have to be brave and say "well, I'm going to get it one way or another and the how will be revealed to me."

At that time, I came back to Spain and I told my parents: "I've decided, I know what I'm going to do, I want to go to Miami, I want to study art direction at an advertising school and it costs $30,000. Can you help me finance my master's degree?" My father replied with a resounding "no."

"Why do you want to go to Miami? All you want to do is party. You're not going to get anything done there. What you should do is go to an advertising agency and work there while you're building your portfolio." This was my dad's reasoning.

This is an important point, when you have a strong, burning desire, like I had, you have to remember that this desire is an agreement that you have between you and the universe. This desire is a seed that you have to take care of, that you have to water and that you have to strengthen.

That little seed that I had, that desire wasn't my father's.

You have to be careful when you share your desires with friends and loved ones because most likely they won't understand or support it. When my father said no, I said to myself: "well, what do we do now?" Because I was counting on my parents to pay for my master's. They paid for my university and they were very generous with that, but now I had to find a way.

I had already made that decision. I was already using my faith. I was taking initiative but I didn't know how I was going to fund it.

Remember that we don't make decisions based on the circumstances in which we are in, we make decisions based on our faith. If I had made a decision based on the circumstances in which I was in, I didn't have $30,000 to pay for the school. I didn't even have money to pay for a ticket to get to the school in Miami.

Instead of worrying or abandoning the desire, what we have to do is connect with our higher mental faculties: imagination, intuition, reasoning, will and perception. I connected with my imagination and kept asking "how can I afford it?"

An idea dropped into my mind: I had my American and Spanish passports. I thought to myself "look at what American students are doing, they are getting loans to go to school. I am American. So, let's see if I could qualify for a loan too."

When you get an idea you must take action immediately because the universe speaks to you through intuition, it gives you ideas and you have to take inspired action based on those ideas.

After my internship in NYC was complete, I went back home to Spain. I was doing my internship at an agency there waiting to hear if I'd qualify for the loans.

And again, the universe gave me another gift. Two weeks before I was going back to the US to celebrate the 50th anniversary of my grandparents in Florida, I received a letter telling me that they had accepted the loan and that they had also given me a partial scholarship.

I made another decision at that moment. The "how" always shows up in the form of opportunities. It occurred to me that since my parents were buying our plane tickets to Tampa for my grandparents 50th anniversary, why not just buy me a one way ticket. It would be cheaper for them and it would get me closer to my dream.

I told my parents about the good news: the loan, wanting to pursue my dream and just getting this one way ticket. My dad wasn't very thrilled with the idea because it wasn't his desire, but I didn't let that stop me.

He did give me the cold shoulder on our way to my grandparents' anniversary. And that was difficult because that's where my fears started to come in again. This time it was the fear of the loss of the love of a loved one, which is my father's love as well as the fear of criticism.

He was rejecting me, I started doubting my decision, but I did remind myself of how strong this desire was. When you have a desire that the universe plants in your heart, you have to remember that it's not anyone else's desire but yours so you can't be guided by the opinions of others unless they are people who have already obtained the same results that you are looking for.

I went to Florida.

We celebrated my grandparents' 50th anniversary. I didn't come back to Spain. Instead I went off to miami.

No Return ticket.

This is important to note because another characteristic of making a quality decision is cutting off all options. The word decision comes from the Latin word decidere.

The syllable cid, means to cut, to kill. That's why the word homicide, suicide, herbicide, pesticide, is all about killing: killing weeds, killing people.

Decidir is cutting all the options you have. Killing all second options.

If I had bought a return ticket, that would have given me another way out.

When I was with my grandparents on their 50th anniversary they sat me down and said "look, we've saved $3,000 from the moment you were born, take the money and succeed." This was so moving because I knew that they didn't have a lot of money and this was huge for them.

I graciously accepted that money, which served me as a deposit for my house rental and to rent a car.

I drove down, I didn't know anyone in Miami. I stayed at a friend's house. I bought a bike and I started looking for a job. I found a job after 10 days in Miami.

I worked for six months before I could start at school because I needed to save some money.

I share all this because with every desire we have, it requires sacrifice. You make a decision and it requires sacrifice: sacrifice of time, money, energy, and feeling uncomfortable. One thing I always tell my clients is "get out of your comfort zone. If you're not doing something that is uncomfortable to you every day, you're not growing, you're just staying in your comfort zone." To grow as a human being, you have to do uncomfortable things, you have to sacrifice.

I would get up at 5 in the morning, ride my bike to work because I didn't have money for a car. I was working as a waitress, and I worked from 6 in the morning until 2 in the afternoon, and from there I would bike to school and leave around 8 or 9pm. They were long days but that was part of the sacrifice. I did that for two years.

Remember, you have the desire, you make the decision, fears arise, you hold on to faith, you take action, and what does the universe give you? It gives you confidence.

When I finished those two years of school at Miami Ad School, I wasn't the same Tania I was two years before. My level of confidence didn't only go up one level, it went up two or three more levels.

When you make such big powerful, scary decisions, the universe gives you so many beautiful things. Six months before I graduated, I already had a job.

The universe gave me my best friend, I met her at Miami Ad School.

The universe gave me my husband. I met my husband at Miami Ad School. And if I hadn't met my husband I wouldn't be here today.

From there I went to work in New York City as an Art Director for multi-million dollar companies like: Starbucks, Nabisco, AT&T, Samsung. I did advertising campaigns for all these people when I was in my twenties.

The course of my life changed because of a decision. I didn't let myself be influenced by the rest of the people –my father and some creative directors who told me that they didn't recommend that school to me.–

Looking back, that decision to pursue my master's degree in Miami was one of the best I've ever made. It taught me invaluable lessons about determination, resilience, and the power of decisive action. It showed me that quality decisions, fueled by passion and backed by unwavering commitment, can transform aspirations into reality.

So, when you find yourself at a crossroads, facing a decision that could potentially change your life, remember this: it's not just about weighing the pros and cons or waiting for the perfect moment. It's about summoning the courage to choose a path and trusting that you have what it takes to navigate the challenges ahead.

Because in the end, it's not the circumstances that define us, but the decisions we make in spite of them. And those decisions, whether big or small, have the power to shape our destinies and lead us towards the fulfillment of our dreams.

The second story about decisions affected us all worldwide.

At the end of 2019 I was so proud of myself because I was only working 20 hours a week, I wasn't on social media and I was able to make more than $100,000 dollars by hosting events and retreats. I couldn't believe it! I was beyond myself. Three months later, COVID hit.

That's when I got that dose of humility, and got sucked in by the collective fear.

Before I mentioned the six ghosts of fear:

- The fear of poverty
- the fear of criticism
- the fear of losing the love of a loved one
- the fear of illness
- the fear of old age and
- the fear of death.

I want you to go back to 2020. That was a collective fear for all of us, but not just one fear, because normally when you make decisions only 1 or 2 fears show up. When Covid hit, the six ghosts of fear came up for most of us. Collectively, we were suffering from all the fears: the fear of poverty, the fear of illness, the fear of death, the fear of criticism. Everything came up for me, and that's when I drifted away, I was lost. I was drifting in 2020 and part of 2021.

In 2021, I made a pivotal decision to change my approach. Instead of focusing solely on local events and retreats for women, I aimed to reach a global audience. This shift was driven by a deep-seated desire in my heart. However, it came with its own set of challenges, particularly financial ones. Despite having previously earned over $100,000, I found myself in significant debt due to unforeseen circumstances affecting my income. To overcome this and achieve my goal of reaching a global audience, I knew I needed to acquire specialized knowledge.

So, I embarked on an intensive learning journey throughout 2021- 2023, akin to pursuing a master's degree. I invested in courses covering public relations, YouTube, marketing, podcasting and got certified as a Master Coach with the Napoleon Hill institute. Additionally, I enlisted the help of an agency to secure opportunities in over 50 podcasts between 2022 and 2023. Despite these efforts, doubts and fears continued to surface, especially when I launched my YouTube channel. Concerns about financial stability and fear of criticism delayed the channel's launch for six months.

Despite these challenges, I pressed on, drawing inspiration from the teachings of Napoleon Hill. Each decision I made—coupled with overcoming fears and maintaining faith—led to increased confidence and opened new doors. One significant outcome was the successful launch of my own podcast, which recently celebrated its first anniversary. The podcast has garnered exceptional success, ranking in the top 1.5% globally with hundreds of five-star reviews and thousands of downloads in just over 14 months.

Now all the fruits that we are starting to see wouldn't be here if I hadn't made that decision to pivot, invest in myself, in acquiring new specialized knowledge and taking action.

My last story about Decision took place two weeks ago.

My daughter stayed home a couple Thursdays ago because she was having a difficult day, but I had an important presentation to finish for an online podcasting summit. It was a tremendous opportunity.

I had to finish this presentation at two in the afternoon on that Thursday. An hour before completion I spotted my daughter in her room crying, – I knew something was up because she's not the type to be throwing tantrums. I went in and said: "Aila, what's wrong? What can I do?" She said something along the lines that no one was paying attention to her and that she wanted me to spend time with her."

I responded "Aila, I can't help you right now. I have a very important presentation to finish"

And she got even more upset and lashed out " that's what happens, no one pays attention to me…" For a split second I debated on what decision to make "Do I take care of my daughter because she's having a difficult time and that's what good moms do or do I decide to finish this presentation that will influence thousands of people who will see it and that it is a tremendous opportunity within the world of podcasting?"

"Mothering or my career?"

What would you have chosen?

Maybe the choice I made was not the right one and each choice would have had different repercussions. I looked at Aila and I said, "we'll talk later, I have to finish up."

I don't know if she will be traumatized, if she will have to go to therapy sessions. I made that decision because doing that presentation was aligned with my definiteness of purpose.

That night, we were hanging out in the hot tub just the two of us –that's our place and time to bond, that's where we soften and connect as mother and daughter. I told Aila: "forgive me for not paying attention to you today when you needed me, when you were crying. But I have to tell you that I was very nervous, I was very anxious, I had to prepare this very important presentation. It was a huge opportunity. And so it was a very difficult decision for me to choose between you and the presentation."

Aila looked at me and said "Mom, what's the best thing that could happen to you because of that presentation?" I was a little stunned thinking "who's the coach here, her or me?"

I finish up with this story because you might be facing some important decisions that you need to make at this time in your life that might make you a bit scared and anxious. As your considering this big decision, I ask you the same thing that my 10 year old asked me: "what's the best thing that could happen?"

Nermin Fathy

CEO & Founder of Papillon

https://www.linkedin.com/company/101869437/admin/feed/posts/
https://www.instagram.com/the.art.of.attire/
https://www.papillonfashions.com

I am a seasoned HR professional with over 15 years of experience in corporate environments, where I dedicated myself to cultivating talent, fostering organizational growth, and championing workplace diversity. Throughout my corporate journey, I discovered a parallel passion for fashion, leading me to pursue formal education and certification as a fashion stylist and fashion designer

Driven by my love for both HR and fashion, I made a bold decision to transition into entrepreneurship, founding my own company specializing in corporate fashion styling. This career shift allowed me to blend my expertise in human resources with my creative flair, helping professionals refine their professional image and align their personal style with their career aspirations.

In addition to my role as a fashion stylist and entrepreneur, I also continue to contribute to the HR field as a consultant and trainer. Drawing from my extensive corporate background, I provide strategic

HR solutions and deliver impactful training programs that empower organizations and individuals to thrive.

My journey from HR professional to certified fashion stylist and entrepreneur reflects my commitment to continuous learning, innovation, and the pursuit of passion-driven career paths. I am passionate about helping individuals harness the power of personal style to enhance their professional presence and achieve their goals in today's competitive business landscape.

The Power of Style: Fashion's Influence on Women Decision-Makers

By Nermin Fathy

Introduction

In today's dynamic and competitive corporate environment, the significance of personal style as a tool for professional success cannot be overstated. For women in leadership roles, fashion serves not only as a means of self-expression but also as a strategic asset that communicates authority, confidence, and individual brand. This chapter explores the profound relationship between fashion styling and decision-making among women leaders, drawing on historical precedents, contemporary examples, and the pivotal role of corporate fashion stylists in empowering women in the workplace.

1. Historical Perspectives

Throughout history, women in positions of power have strategically used fashion to assert authority, influence public perception, and convey political messages. Queen Elizabeth I of England, known for her elaborate and symbolic attire, employed fashion as a potent tool of statecraft. Her meticulously designed gowns and intricate accessories not only showcased her wealth and status but also communicated messages of power, patriotism, and divine right to rule.

Similarly, Coco Chanel revolutionized women's fashion in the early 20th century, liberating them from restrictive clothing and empowering them to express independence and professionalism through her timeless designs.

In more recent times, figures like Jacqueline Kennedy Onassis exemplified elegance and sophistication through her timeless fashion choices. As

First Lady of the United States during the 1960s, she became a global fashion icon by promoting American designers and setting trends that reflected her grace, poise, and cultural diplomacy. Her influence extended beyond fashion to shaping public perception and supporting the arts.

Books such as *Women Who Run with the Wolves* by Clarissa Pinkola Estés explore the symbolic power of women's clothing choices throughout history. Estés argues that clothing serves as a form of armor, enabling women to navigate societal expectations while asserting their individuality and reclaiming their power. By embracing their unique fashion statements, women throughout history have challenged norms and reshaped cultural narratives.

Books such as *The Power of style* by Annette Tapert and Diana Edkins explore the intersection of fashion and power through historical anecdotes and insightful analyses of influential women. The authors highlight how fashion can be a tool for empowerment, allowing women to navigate societal expectations and assert their individuality in the public sphere.

2. Contemporary Insights

In today's globalized and digitally connected world, female leaders continue to leverage fashion as a means of personal branding and professional assertion. Michelle Obama, during her tenure as First Lady, redefined the role of fashion in politics by championing diverse designers and embracing accessible yet sophisticated attire. Her wardrobe choices not only reflected her personal style but also conveyed messages of inclusivity, cultural pride, and advocacy for social causes.

In *Lean In: Women, Work, and the Will to Lead*, Sheryl Sandberg explores the nuances of appearance and attire in professional settings. Sandberg acknowledges the double standards that women often face regarding their appearance but emphasizes the importance of authenticity and self-expression in achieving professional success. She argues that by owning their unique style, women can challenge stereotypes and redefine leadership standards.

Sheryl Sandberg discusses the importance of appearance in professional settings, acknowledging the double standards that women often face regarding their attire. Sandberg argues that while appearance should not dictate a woman's worth or competence, it undeniably plays a role in shaping perceptions and influencing professional opportunities.

Sandberg's insights underscore the importance of authenticity and self-expression in navigating corporate environments while challenging traditional gender norms.

Magazines such as *Vogue* and *Harper's Bazaar* regularly feature profiles and interviews with influential women who exemplify the intersection of fashion and leadership. Articles delve into how CEOs, entrepreneurs, and public figures strategically use fashion to enhance their professional image, communicate their values, and inspire confidence among stakeholders.

3. The Role of Corporate Fashion Stylists

Behind every polished image of a woman in leadership lies the expertise of corporate fashion stylists. These professionals possess a deep understanding of fashion trends, personal branding, and the psychological impact of attire on perception. As a corporate fashion stylist with over a decade of experience, I've witnessed firsthand the transformative power of wardrobe consultations and styling sessions for women executives.

These professionals play a pivotal role in enhancing the visual narrative of women executives through strategic wardrobe curation and styling advice tailored to individual personalities and professional goals.

Corporate fashion stylists collaborate closely with their clients to understand their brand identity and career aspirations. They curate wardrobes that not only align with the organization's culture and dress code but also reflect the executive's personal style and leadership persona. By selecting clothing that emphasizes fit, color palette, and fabric quality, stylists help women executives project confidence and professionalism in every professional interaction.

As a corporate fashion stylist with extensive experience, I've had the privilege of working with women leaders across various industries to refine their visual presence and enhance their professional impact. Through personalized consultations and styling sessions, I've witnessed firsthand how the right wardrobe choices can empower women to overcome barriers, assert their authority, and make informed decisions that drive organizational success.

3.1 Bobbi Brown

In *The Power of Style: A Personal Journey*, Bobbi Brown shares insights into the role of appearance in personal and professional success. As a makeup artist and entrepreneur, Brown emphasizes the importance of confidence and authenticity in cultivating a signature style that resonates with one's audience and empowers women to navigate competitive industries. She advocates for embracing one's natural beauty and using makeup and fashion as tools for self-expression and empowerment.

Here are additional examples of influential figures and their perspectives on fashion and personal branding:

3.2 Stacy London

Stacy London is a renowned stylist and television personality known for her role on the show *What not to Wear*. She has written extensively about the transformative power of fashion and how style impacts confidence and professional success. London's approach emphasizes the importance of understanding one's body type, personal preferences, and how clothing can be used to convey a strong, authentic image.

3.3 Giovanna Battaglia Engelbert

Giovanna Battaglia Engelbert is an Italian fashion editor and creative director known for her bold and eclectic style. As a prominent figure in the fashion industry, Engelbert's approach to styling blends high fashion with personal flair, demonstrating how confidence and creativity can elevate one's professional presence.

3.4 Rachel Zoe

Rachel Zoe is a celebrity stylist and fashion designer who has built a successful career by helping clients, including prominent women in entertainment and business, define and refine their personal style. Zoe's insights into fashion emphasize the importance of self-expression and using clothing as a tool for empowerment and confidence.

These figures offer diverse perspectives on the role of fashion in personal branding and professional success, showcasing how different approaches to styling can empower women to assert their authority and make impactful decisions in their careers. Integrating their insights into the chapter can provide a broader understanding of how fashion influences leadership and decision-making among women in various industries.

4. Fashion as a Tool for Influence

Beyond aesthetics, fashion serves as a strategic tool for influencing perceptions, fostering connections, and communicating leadership qualities. The psychology of clothing choice reveals how attire can convey professionalism, approachability, and adaptability—qualities essential for effective decision-making and leadership. By strategically curating their wardrobes, women executives not only enhance their personal brand but also establish credibility and inspire trust among colleagues and stakeholders.

4.1 Enhancing Professional Presence

Fashion plays a pivotal role in enhancing professional presence and projecting leadership qualities. The psychology of clothing choice reveals how attire can convey professionalism, approachability, and adaptability—essential qualities for effective decision-making and leadership. For women in leadership roles, wardrobe choices are not just about looking good but also about communicating confidence and authority.

Stacy London, a renowned stylist and television personality, emphasizes the transformative power of fashion in boosting self-esteem and enhancing professional impact. Through her work on *What not to wear*, London has shown how strategic wardrobe choices can empower individuals to command respect and credibility in professional settings. By aligning their appearance with their leadership goals, women executives can create a strong first impression and establish a lasting presence in their organizations.

4.2 Communicating Values and Identity

Fashion serves as a visual language through which women leaders can communicate their values, beliefs, and identity to stakeholders and peers. Christine Centenera, a fashion stylist and editor, exemplifies this approach through her minimalist yet avant-garde style. Centenera's fashion choices not only reflect her individuality but also convey a sense of confidence and creativity that resonates with her professional persona.

Corporate fashion stylists play a crucial role in assisting women executives in crafting a cohesive and authentic personal brand through their wardrobe. By understanding the organizational culture and strategic goals of their clients, stylists curate outfits that align with the executive's leadership style while maintaining professionalism and elegance. This strategic approach allows women leaders to navigate complex professional environments with confidence and clarity.

4.3 Influence and Persuasion

Robert B. Cialdini, in his book *Influence: The Psychology of Persuasion*, explores how appearance and attire contribute to influencing perceptions and decisions. Cialdini argues that by consciously managing their appearance, individuals can establish credibility, authority, and trustworthiness among colleagues and stakeholders. For women decision-makers, strategic wardrobe choices can enhance their persuasive influence and enable them to effectively communicate their vision and goals.

4.4 Building Connections and Networks

Fashion also plays a crucial role in building connections and networks within professional circles. Dressing appropriately for various business events, from conferences to networking dinners, can facilitate meaningful interactions and open doors to new opportunities. Women leaders who invest in their professional appearance demonstrate respect for themselves and others, signaling their commitment to success and collaboration.

In *Influence: The Psychology of Persuasion* Robert B. Cialdini explores principles of influence, including the role of appearance in shaping initial impressions and establishing authority. Cialdini's research underscores the power of visual cues in influencing others' perceptions and decisions, highlighting the importance of intentional styling in professional success. He argues that by aligning their appearance with their leadership goals, women can enhance their persuasive influence and achieve greater impact in their organizations.

5. Challenges and Innovations

Despite significant strides toward gender equality, women decision-makers often face unique challenges in navigating fashion expectations, stereotypes, and societal biases. The pressure to balance authenticity with professionalism can be daunting, particularly in male-dominated industries where traditional norms of attire prevail. However, innovative approaches in corporate fashion styling offer solutions by promoting diversity, inclusivity, and creativity in wardrobe choices.

In *Women in Clothes*, Sheila Heti, Heidi Julavits, and Leanne Shapton compile a diverse collection of essays and interviews that explore the complex relationship between women, clothing, and identity. The anthology features personal narratives and cultural critiques that challenge conventional notions of fashion and empower women to embrace their individuality through style. Contributors share their experiences of using fashion as a form of self-expression, resistance, and empowerment in various social and professional contexts.

6. Fashion and Social Contexts

The anthology delves into how clothing intersects with various social contexts, such as work environments, family dynamics, and cultural traditions. Examples from the book can illustrate how women navigate these contexts through their fashion choices, balancing personal expression with societal expectations

6.1 Work Environments

Clothing plays a crucial role in work environments, where professional attire often sets the tone for credibility and competence. Women decision-makers navigate workplace dress codes while balancing personal style and professional expectations. For instance, *Women in Clothes* features narratives of women executives who strategically choose attire that commands respect without sacrificing individuality. These examples illustrate how fashion can empower women to project authority and leadership in male-dominated industries.

6.2 Family Dynamics

Fashion choices can also reflect cultural and familial expectations. In multicultural societies, women leaders may integrate traditional attire with modern styles to honor their heritage while asserting their professional identity. The anthology explores how women negotiate these dual identities through clothing, showcasing stories of resilience and cultural pride. For example, contributors discuss the significance of clothing in family rituals and celebrations, highlighting how attire serves as a link between past traditions and contemporary roles.

6.3 Cultural Traditions

Across cultures, clothing serves as a powerful marker of identity and social status. The book examines how women leaders navigate cultural norms through their fashion choices, addressing issues of modesty, symbolism, and respect. For instance, in conservative business environments, women may adapt their wardrobe to convey professionalism while adhering to cultural modesty standards. These narratives offer insights into the nuanced ways that fashion intersects with cultural heritage and professional success.

7. Fashion, Identity, and Empowerment

Fashion is a powerful medium through which individuals express their unique identities and assert their personal empowerment. It serves as a canvas for self-expression, allowing people to convey their values, beliefs, and aspirations through their choice of attire. By curating their own style, individuals can challenge societal norms and embrace their true selves, ultimately fostering a sense of confidence and empowerment.

7.1 Fashion as a Tool for Self-Expression and Identity Formation

Fashion serves as a powerful vehicle for women decision-makers to express their individuality, creativity, and personal values. Clothing choices allow them to communicate their unique perspectives and assert their identity within professional spheres. For example, a CEO known for her bold color choices and avant-garde accessories may use fashion to convey innovation and risk-taking in business strategies. By aligning their wardrobe with their personal ethos, women leaders establish a cohesive narrative that resonates with their stakeholders and inspires trust and admiration.

7.2 Communicating Values, Beliefs, and Leadership Qualities

Clothing can subtly communicate a leader's values, beliefs, and leadership qualities to colleagues, clients, and the public. A philanthropic entrepreneur may prioritize ethically sourced materials and sustainable fashion practices, reflecting her commitment to social responsibility and environmental stewardship. Through conscious fashion choices, women decision-makers signal their dedication to causes greater than profit margins, fostering a corporate culture of integrity and empathy.

7.3 Case Studies of Trailblazing Women

Across industries, women have challenged traditional fashion norms to redefine leadership standards and inspire positive change. For instance, Angela Ahrendts, former CEO of Burberry and Senior Vice President at Apple, transformed both companies with her visionary leadership and impeccable style. Ahrendts' approach to fashion fused luxury with technology, signaling a new era of innovation in retail and tech industries.

In the entertainment industry, Oprah Winfrey has used her media platform and distinctive style to advocate for social justice and empower women worldwide. Winfrey's signature look, often characterized by bold colors and statement jewelry, reflects her confidence and commitment to uplifting marginalized voices. Through her philanthropic efforts and media presence, Winfrey has redefined the narrative of success and leadership for women of all backgrounds.

8. Fashion as a Strategic Asset

Fashion is a powerful tool that women leaders strategically leverage to enhance their professional image, influence perceptions, and align with organizational goals and values. Beyond mere attire, clothing choices wield significant influence in shaping workplace dynamics, fostering confidence, and communicating leadership qualities.

In the realm of leadership and decision-making, fashion is not merely a matter of personal style; it is a strategic tool that women executives wield to enhance their professional presence, communicate their values, and influence perceptions within their industries.

8.1 Influencing Perceptions and Attitudes in the Workplace

Clothing choices play a crucial role in shaping how women decision-makers are perceived by colleagues, clients, and stakeholders in the workplace. A well-curated wardrobe that aligns with professional expectations can project competence, credibility, and authority. For example, a tailored suit or a polished dress can signal seriousness and attention to detail, instilling confidence in leadership capabilities. Conversely, fashion-forward attire may convey innovation and forward-thinking, positioning women leaders as creative visionaries within their industries.

Perceptions influenced by fashion extend beyond professionalism; they also encompass cultural sensitivity and inclusivity. Women leaders who adapt their wardrobe to reflect diverse cultural norms demonstrate respect and understanding, fostering a positive and inclusive work environment. By aligning fashion choices with organizational values of diversity and inclusivity, leaders not only inspire trust but also strengthen corporate culture and employee morale.

8.2 Psychological Impact of Attire on Self-Confidence and Assertiveness

The psychological effects of attire on self-confidence and assertiveness are profound for women decision-makers. Research shows that dressing well can enhance mood, increase self-esteem, and boost cognitive performance in professional settings. A carefully chosen outfit that makes a woman feel empowered and comfortable can significantly impact her demeanor and interactions with others.

Moreover, attire influences how others perceive one's competence and leadership potential. Studies indicate that individuals dressed in formal attire are often perceived as more competent and authoritative than their casually dressed counterparts. This phenomenon, known as "enclothed cognition," suggests that clothing affects not only how others see us but also how we see ourselves.

Understanding the psychological nuances of attire allows women leaders to harness fashion as a tool for self-empowerment and leadership development. By selecting outfits that evoke confidence and professionalism, they can enhance their executive presence and command respect in professional environments.

8.3 Enhancing Professional Presence

Clothing choices play a pivotal role in shaping how women decision-makers are perceived in the workplace. A meticulously curated wardrobe can convey competence, credibility, and authority. For instance, a tailored suit or a sophisticated dress can project professionalism and command respect in boardroom meetings and client presentations. By aligning their attire with the organizational culture and expectations, women leaders establish a visual identity that reinforces their leadership role and fosters trust among stakeholders.

8.4 Communicating Values and Leadership Qualities

Fashion serves as a non-verbal communication tool through which women leaders express their values, beliefs, and leadership qualities. For example, a CEO known for her commitment to sustainability may prioritize eco-friendly fashion brands and materials in her wardrobe choices. This aligns with her corporate ethos and communicates a dedication to environmental stewardship to employees, investors, and consumers alike. By integrating their personal values into their fashion choices, women decision-makers cultivate an authentic and transparent leadership style that resonates with stakeholders and inspires loyalty.

8.5 Building Brand Identity

Fashion plays a crucial role in shaping a leader's personal brand and professional reputation. A distinctive and consistent style can differentiate women executives in competitive industries and position them as thought leaders and innovators. For instance, a tech entrepreneur may adopt a minimalist and futuristic wardrobe that reflects her company's cutting-edge approach to technology and design. By leveraging fashion as a branding tool, women decision-makers create a cohesive narrative that reinforces their expertise, vision, and industry influence.

8.6 Navigating Cultural and Social Contexts

In multicultural and globalized business environments, fashion helps women leaders navigate diverse cultural norms and social expectations. A diplomatic ambassador or international business executive may adapt their wardrobe to respect local customs and traditions while maintaining their professional identity. By demonstrating cultural sensitivity through clothing choices, women decision-makers build rapport, foster cross-cultural understanding, and facilitate productive business relationships on a global scale.

8.7 Strategic Impact on Organizational Culture

Fashion choices can influence organizational culture by setting standards for professionalism, creativity, and inclusivity. A forward-thinking CEO who embraces diversity and innovation may encourage employees to express their individuality through dress while adhering to workplace guidelines. By fostering a culture that celebrates diverse fashion expressions, women leaders promote creativity, morale, and a sense of belonging among team members. This inclusive approach enhances employee engagement and organizational productivity, driving sustainable growth and success.

8.8 Case Studies of Strategic Fashion Leadership

Numerous case studies illustrate how women decision-makers strategically leverage fashion to achieve business objectives and drive organizational success. For example, Indra Nooyi, former CEO of PepsiCo, was known for her distinctive style that blended elegance with corporate sophistication. Nooyi's fashion choices reinforced her global leadership stature and commitment to diversity and sustainability in the beverage industry.

Another example is Angela Ahrendts, former CEO of Burberry and Senior Vice President at Apple, whose visionary leadership and impeccable style transformed both companies. Ahrendts' strategic approach to fashion marketing and retail innovation propelled Burberry into a global luxury brand and revolutionized Apple's retail experience. Her fashion-forward initiatives, such as digital runway shows and immersive store designs, reshaped industry standards and elevated customer engagement.

Michelle Obama, Former First Lady of the United States: Michelle Obama's fashion diplomacy during her tenure as First Lady exemplified strategic fashion leadership. She championed American designers and celebrated diversity in fashion, using her wardrobe to promote inclusivity and cultural diplomacy on the global stage. Her fashion choices, characterized by elegance and accessibility, resonated with audiences worldwide and reinforced her advocacy for social causes.

These case studies highlight how women leaders strategically integrate fashion into their leadership narratives, aligning personal style with organizational values to drive innovation, inspire stakeholders, and foster a positive corporate culture.

9. Future Trends and Outlook

As society evolves, so too does the intersection of fashion and women's leadership, presenting new opportunities and challenges for aspiring and current women decision-makers. Looking ahead, several key trends and considerations are shaping the future landscape of fashion in leadership.

9.1 Predictions for the Future Role of Fashion in Shaping Women's Leadership Styles

Fashion will continue to play a pivotal role in shaping women's leadership styles, evolving beyond traditional norms to embrace diversity, inclusivity, and authenticity. Future leaders are likely to leverage fashion as a strategic tool to communicate their values, amplify their voices, and inspire change within their organizations and communities.

Inclusive Fashion Representation: There will be a growing emphasis on diverse representation in fashion media and leadership narratives. Women leaders from various backgrounds and identities will redefine beauty standards and challenge industry norms through their unique styles and perspectives.

Tech-Integrated Fashion: The integration of technology in fashion will revolutionize how women leaders engage with their audiences and stakeholders. Wearable technology, smart fabrics, and virtual fashion experiences will enhance personalization and sustainability in fashion choices, aligning with innovative leadership practices.

Gender-Neutral Fashion: The future of fashion in leadership will likely see a shift towards gender-neutral styles that promote equality and inclusivity in professional settings. Leaders will embrace fluidity in fashion choices to reflect evolving societal attitudes towards gender expression and identity.

9.2 Analysis of Emerging Trends in Sustainable Fashion and Implications for Women Decision Makers

Sustainable fashion will increasingly shape women's leadership styles, driven by a global movement towards environmental responsibility and ethical consumption. Aspiring and current women leaders can harness sustainable fashion practices to align their personal values with organizational goals and drive positive change:

Circular Economy Initiatives: Leaders will advocate for circular economy principles in fashion, promoting recycling, upcycling, and waste reduction in supply chains. Women decision-makers can pioneer eco-friendly initiatives that prioritize sustainable materials and ethical production practices, thereby setting industry benchmarks for corporate responsibility.

Ethical Fashion Advocacy: There will be a heightened focus on ethical fashion advocacy, with leaders using their platforms to champion transparency, fair labor practices, and social justice in the fashion industry. By partnering with ethical brands and supporting sustainable fashion initiatives, women leaders can inspire consumer confidence and foster a culture of ethical leadership.

Impact Investing in Fashion: Impact investing will emerge as a strategic approach for women decision-makers to support sustainable fashion startups and initiatives. Leaders can leverage their influence and resources to fund innovative solutions that address environmental challenges and promote social equity within the fashion ecosystem.

9.3 Recommendations for Aspiring Leaders on Harnessing the Power of Style

For aspiring leaders looking to harness the power of style to achieve professional goals and make a lasting impact, the following recommendations can guide their journey:

Define Your Personal Brand: Clarify your values, strengths, and leadership goals to develop a cohesive personal brand that aligns with your professional aspirations. Use fashion as a tool to express your unique identity and communicate your leadership qualities to stakeholders.

Stay Informed About Fashion Trends: Stay abreast of emerging fashion trends, industry developments, and cultural shifts that influence leadership styles. Incorporate elements of current fashion trends into your wardrobe while maintaining authenticity and professionalism.

Invest in Quality and Versatility: Prioritize quality craftsmanship and versatile pieces that can transition seamlessly from professional settings to networking events and public appearances. Build a wardrobe that reflects your confidence, competence, and readiness to lead.

Embrace Sustainability: Embrace sustainable fashion practices by supporting ethical brands, opting for eco-friendly materials, and minimizing your fashion footprint. Lead by example in promoting sustainability within your organization and industry.

Network and Collaborate: Network with fashion influencers, industry leaders, and mentors who can provide guidance and opportunities for professional growth. Collaborate with like-minded individuals and organizations to amplify your impact and advocate for positive change through fashion leadership.

10. Empowerment through Fashion: Embracing Intersectionality

Fashion serves as a potent tool for expressing and celebrating intersectional identities, promoting both personal empowerment and societal change. It provides a platform where diverse voices can be amplified, fostering inclusivity and challenging conventional norms. Fashion is not merely an act of adorning oneself; it is a dynamic form of expression that intersects with various aspects of identity, including race, gender, sexuality, and culture. Recognizing these intersections is crucial in understanding how fashion can both empower and marginalize. Through thoughtful fashion choices, individuals navigate and assert their complex identities in ways that challenge societal norms and promote self-empowerment. In the ever-evolving landscape of fashion, leaders have a unique responsibility to champion inclusivity and diversity.

10.1 Intersectional Identities and Fashion Choices

Intersectionality refers to the interconnected nature of social categorizations such as race, gender, ethnicity, socioeconomic status, and more, which can create overlapping and interdependent systems of discrimination or disadvantage. In the realm of fashion leadership, intersectional identities profoundly influence individuals' fashion choices and leadership approaches.

Cultural Heritage and Style Expression: Women leaders from diverse cultural backgrounds often integrate elements of their heritage into their fashion choices, celebrating their cultural identity while challenging stereotypes and expanding fashion norms. For example, a Latina CEO may incorporate vibrant colors and traditional patterns into her professional wardrobe, showcasing pride in her cultural heritage.

Gender Expression and Fashion Freedom: Gender-nonconforming and transgender leaders may navigate fashion choices that align with their gender identity, advocating for inclusivity and challenging gender norms within corporate environments. Fashion becomes a tool for self-expression and empowerment, enabling leaders to authentically represent their identities while promoting acceptance and respect.

Body Positivity and Representation: Leaders who embrace body positivity advocate for diverse body types and sizes in fashion leadership. They may collaborate with inclusive fashion brands that offer a wide range of sizes and designs, challenging industry standards and promoting confidence and self-esteem among consumers and employees alike.

10.2 Recommendations for Promoting Inclusivity and Diversity through Fashion Leadership

Promoting inclusivity and diversity within fashion leadership requires intentional efforts to amplify marginalized voices, challenge stereotypes, and create equitable opportunities. Here are recommendations for advancing inclusivity through fashion leadership:

Educational Initiatives: Incorporate diversity and inclusion training into fashion education programs and leadership development courses. Educate future leaders on the importance of cultural sensitivity, representation, and equity in fashion decision-making.

Collaborative Partnerships: Foster partnerships with diverse fashion designers, influencers, and community leaders to co-create inclusive fashion collections and campaigns. Collaborate with organizations that promote social justice and advocate for underrepresented communities in the fashion industry.

Visibility and Representation: Feature diverse models, executives, and leaders in fashion campaigns, editorials, and runway shows. Highlight intersectional identities and celebrate individuality to reflect the diversity of global audiences and consumer demographics.

Policy and Advocacy: Advocate for inclusive policies and practices within fashion companies, such as non-discrimination policies, accessible fashion options, and inclusive marketing strategies. Champion diversity in hiring practices and leadership positions to create a more inclusive industry culture.

Consumer Engagement: Engage with consumers through transparent communication about ethical sourcing, sustainability practices, and commitment to diversity. Empower consumers to make informed purchasing decisions that support brands aligned with their values of inclusivity and social responsibility.

In conclusion, the dynamic interplay between fashion and leadership illuminates a powerful narrative of self-expression, empowerment, and cultural resonance among women decision-makers. As we traverse the ever-evolving landscape of fashion leadership, it becomes evident that clothing is not merely a fabric draped on shoulders but a canvas through which leaders assert their values, challenge norms, and inspire change. By embracing inclusivity, celebrating diversity, and advocating for ethical practices, fashion leaders forge paths of innovation and equity in their industries. Aspiring leaders are encouraged to harness the transformative power of style, recognizing it not only as a reflection of personal identity but as a strategic tool to redefine success and shape a future where leadership is as diverse and multifaceted as the styles that adorn it.

Megan Waite

Founder of Megan Waite Coaching

https://www.linkedin.com/in/meganwaite/
https://www.facebook.com/meganwaitecoaching
https://www.instagram.com/meganwaitecoaching/
http://www.meganwaite.com/
https://meganwaitecoaching.com/

I used to suck at making decisions. My parents even gave me a book in highschool on how to make decisions. Well, it didn't help. I still didn't feel worthy and didn't value myself enough to make the best decisions for me. I entered a career helping people make great decisions for themselves. Ironic right? Meanwhile, I continued to make crappy decisions for me. What gives? I finally boiled it down. Take the emotion out of making the best decision for myself, easily and quickly in only 7 steps. Now I have been making decisions that have turned my life around. I'm a busy Mom of 4 kids, I run my own company and I'm proud to say I have coached thousands of people over the years as they made decisions that improved their lives. Ready to join them? Say "YES" to you! Follow me over to my chapter now.

Using Your Go Power for Decision-Making

By Megan Waite

Hey, powerful decision-maker! Yeah, I'm talking to you. What? Not feeling like the powerful female decision-maker you truly are? Well, I totally get it. I felt the same way for over half of my life. Sometimes, I was scared. Sometimes, I was confused. Sometimes, I just felt too defeated and beaten down. I was always so worried about what other people thought or what others wanted that was different from myself. I wanted to make people happy. I was also afraid of making a mistake. What if I made the wrong decision? How long would it be before I even realized I had made the wrong decision? So much uncertainty, a lack of belief in myself, and a history of making bad decisions had led me to default to what other people wanted instead of what I wanted. Can you relate to any of this?

Ironically, despite being a terrible decision-maker for myself in my personal life, I was actually kick-ass at helping other people make great decisions for themselves in my career. Crazy, right? Why was this? Why was I so great at helping my clients make better decisions for themselves, yet I continued to struggle in my own day-to-day life with making decisions best suited for me and my personal desires and goals?

THE QUESTION

As I searched for the answer to why I could help other people better than myself, I looked back at this dichotomy throughout my career and college years. I recognized that in college, I was trained to follow certain protocols and procedures with clients depending on their specific ailments in combination with where they were starting from during our initial evaluation session. I should pause and preface that I was a physical therapist in the healthcare world for over 20 years. People came to me with all sorts of issues happening in their bodies that they could not fix, or they could not decide on what to do next to achieve their desired goal or outcome. This is where I shined. It was rare that I could not help a client achieve progress towards their goals and typically reach not only their short-term goals related to their bodies within a few days to a few weeks but also their much bigger long-term goals.

Helping others reach their goals is so rewarding to me. Due to my career in healthcare, I recognize that the human body is quite a genius problem-solving machine. Given the right tools, procedures, and the right time frame, paired with some personal awareness of our own habits, even our individual make-or-break non-negotiables, we are each gifted with our own genius problem-solving machines. Therefore, we women also possess these genius problem-solving machines and are very capable of making great decisions for ourselves. We women simply train ourselves at a young age to ignore our body's signs and symptoms in exchange for forcing ahead and taking care of everyone else's needs before our own. Sound familiar? Well, it's time to take back our own power and return to using this beautiful decision-making machine for our own personal benefit. It's time to raise your staph and declare, "I am important too!"

Our decisions have a huge impact on our lives, the lives around us, and outward into our world. There is no reason that we should not also benefit from the decisions we make for ourselves. It's time to take ownership of not just the big decisions in your life but even the small day-to-day decisions that compound and lead you to the place you may or may not be happy about right now. What if taking charge of your own decision-making process could change both the current landscape of your life and also the future life that you are currently working towards creating? If you are not making decisions that allow you to dream bigger and you feel stuck in a rut of dreaming small and staying small, we need to chat. If you are anything like my old self and you do not trust your decision-making machine, then you are in the right place, my friend. Let the fun begin! It's time to dream BIG!

DREAM BIG

Your own decision-making process will certainly take some practice, and many of us could use some added support. I used to be very resistant to support, especially when I felt it was something I should know how to do myself. Making good decisions seems like it should be easy, shouldn't it? It seems like a "fail" if you need support, but that is not true. The reality and my personal history point to the fact that just like support with making decisions in your own personal healthcare, support in improving your own personal decision-making method could mean the difference between reaching your goals and maybe not reaching them at all.

Support lends itself to stronger focus with the larger opportunity of achieving your goals set as you re-evaluate and redirect your decisions with support along the way. This same step-by-step process I used in the medical field translates to making great decisions for ourselves on a daily basis. If the human body knows how to solve the issue most of the time and heal itself with or without support, so can we women!

We can heal ourselves by making better decisions. Decisions that have a positive, not negative or negligent impact on our lives. Let's first decide to put our wants, needs, and desires first, even if it's just playfully for the fun of it, and see what becomes. So, is it agreed that all of us women have access to our own genius problem-solving machines? If you are not convinced, it's okay. Just keep going. Proof is always in the pudding, and it's smart to test the theory before you buy it.

Now you may be asking yourself, what if the tug of sickness or pain is not there? Does this same decision-making procedure still work if you are starting from a lesser place of pain? Well, I, too, was curious. I did some research, and over 10 years ago, I went on to become trained as a Health & Wellness Coach to add more of a wellness and coaching element to my healthcare practice. After my training was completed, I sat with the very first cohort and passed the National Board Certification for Health & Wellness Coaches in the US. Since then, I've coached thousands of clients in bettering their lives. I did not use a medical model decision-making process, but a wellness model, and guess what? The same decision-making process surfaced and repeatedly proved itself to be true and duplicatable.

This all sounds great in the name of health, wellness, and healthcare, but what about other areas of life? Will this decision-making model translate to other areas of interest? Great question. My ever-curious mind had this same question, too. Let's fast-forward to only three years ago when I was ready for yet another change in my life.

DREAM BIGGER

Yes, once I understood and started actively practicing this decision-making method for myself, I started dreaming even bigger. I got to work and created my life in alignment with my values and always expanding desires. I started digging into something totally out of my box, real estate investing. Real estate investing appeared both interesting and lucrative. I took an educational course and teamed up with some real movers and shakers in the industry. I did well and grew my business quickly. The company brought me on to help coach their students in making the best decisions for themselves in order to be most successful with the real estate investing program. Again, I recognized that there was a clear, repeatable process to help move people from where they were starting to where they wanted to be in the near future. The students started dreaming bigger than they thought possible. The same structured path I used in both healthcare and wellness coaching proved to be yet again true. This included making deliberate, focused decisions in a step-by-step process with a goal of bettering their own lives and the lives of those around them in the topic of real estate investing.

YOU HOLD THE POWER

After thirty years of assessing and implementing what truly works for people of all demographics, topics, and situations to make great decisions, I've concluded that it boils down to seven specific elements. When these seven elements are used in a sequential order to make deliberate and focused decisions, it can equate to lasting change. More specifically, lasting, wanted, positive, purposeful change. These same seven steps can be applied to both day-to-day decisions and even those big, difficult, life-changing decisions. This is a duplicatable and repeatable method.

I started using this method myself in both my daily life and with my more emotionally driven and critical life-pivoting decisions. And guess what? It turns out that we ALL (even ME!) hold the power to make great decisions. I'm serious. We ALL, including you, have what it takes to make great decisions for ourselves and the life we want to live. Sounds almost too good to be true, right? Well, we already know these simple seven elements (just like the body knows how to heal itself), and when placed in a procedural order, this decision-making method removes the emotion, and you come to the best decision for you. Now, I get it, I am no fool. There is certainly a lot of emotion that can go into making decisions, so using a very focused, clear step-by-step method, removes the fear, uncertainty, wishful thinking, and all the other non-serving emotions from the equation so that you can focus on what is most important: achieving your desired goal.

Are you jumping around a little bit inside? Ready to know these simple seven steps so you, too, can start making the best decisions for yourself? I am so ready to unveil this time-tested method that has worked for both myself and thousands of women, just like us. Grab your pen and notebook or if you are less old school, maybe hit voice record, take a screenshot, or type on your tablet. Honestly, I do not care how you record these simple seven steps. In fact, I turned them into an easy-to-remember phrase so that you will NEVER forget them! Here it comes... Sound the horn! Big Inhale... Let's tap into your personal simple seven decision-making method called ... GO POWER! Now exhale. Can you feel it? GO POWER! Really, Meg? GO POWER? Come on. It sounds like something my kid would watch on television. You can't be serious?

Alright, take it easy. It sounds simple, right? Well, it is truly this simple. The simple seven in sequential order is G-O-P-O-W-E-R. Speaking for myself, we women may sometimes overcomplicate things (probably an understatement). Do you ever do that? I've been known to do this on one too many occasions. I might even be the queen of taking simple concepts and making them highly complicated. Who knows, maybe lifetimes ago, I was Socrates or another well-known philosopher and I overthink everything. Anyway, you get my point. Let's keep this already anxiety-provoking topic of decision-making as simple, duplicatable, and successful as possible. SO, why not a quick and easy acronym to help us stay focused?

GO POWER is a simple phrase that will help you quickly and easily navigate through all the forcefields you are trying to deflect while you harness your spiraling mind and focus on making the best decision for you. Stay with me as we follow these simple seven steps to quickly arrive at the best decision for you, no matter what your topic.

YOUR SUPPORT

Come on. Take my hand. Go ahead. Grab it. My hand is soft. Maybe I have a few wrinkles setting in, and some aging spots are forming, regardless, take my hand and let me walk you through each step. By the end of this chapter, you will have a good grasp on how to harness and use your Go Power, the "simple seven", to make your decisions the best decisions for you. If you want more personal support and hand-holding because you are in a moment of panic or crisis when you don't know what to do, I'm here to help. Even if it's just for your first few times using this method, I'm here for you. Now keep in mind that muscle memory does not occur from reading one single chapter once. To get a deep dive and build positive habitual patterns, after this book, jump on over to www.MeganWaiteCoching.com, where we can stay connected, and you can get more practice and support using your Go Power beyond this chapter.

TRY IT ON

Now, close your eyes for just a minute. Let's try it on. Try on your new Go Power, even though you do not really understand what it is yet. You soon will have your big Ah-Ha moment. You will feel your Go Power coming together to support you each day as you face your daily decisions on topics that are important to you. You may even have a big decision you are facing right now while reading this chapter. Your Go Power is built to handle all types of decisions and will not fail you. Your Go Power is yours and only yours. You can keep it a secret or share it with someone you trust. You can even share it from the mountain tops because, as my 5-year-old says, "Sharing is caring!" But first, let's learn what each element of this decision-making method stands for so you can practice using it for yourself before sharing it with others.

Let's step into your GO POWER. Let's GO! The "G" stands for GENIUS. You ARE a true GENIUS. We already talked about how your body is a genius healing machine. Your cells naturally want homeostasis, so your body is always naturally self-correcting to find its happy place. Pair your body's natural intelligence with your personal inside information on your own desires, likes, and dislikes and you are now making the best decisions for you and you alone. You are the chooser, the decider, the creator of your life, and if something is not going the way you want it to go, then what it takes is already inside of you to make the choice to make a change.

YOU ARE GENIUS

You are a genius! You are powerful. You are worthy. Your decisions do matter. Your decisions impact you fully and the life you are living. It is so important to remember and truly know that YOU and only YOU have full control, full power over your biggest and even smallest life decisions.

You are the genius behind your story. No one else can choose for you. Well, at least you truly should not want others to choose for you. This is how people find themselves (including myself early on) in bad situations, having decided to NOT make the decision and let others make the decision for you. The outcome is typically never in your favor or your best interest. It might be painted that way, but that's not really how it lands. How would someone else know all your values, wants, desires, and goals to make the best decision for you? Maybe it comes from a good place. I know I've done this many times as a Mom for my teenage children. I have overcared to the point where I was making decisions for them, but it had a twist of me in the decision-making process, therefore, it was not always the best decision for them, and the outcome was skewed. So first, take back your own Power and say "yes" to listening to your own genius self when making decisions.

So step one, "**G**", stands for **G**enius. It's all about reclaiming your own genius and getting into the right mindset. You are the true genius behind the decisions you have made in your life, even if they do not feel so genius looking back. But this is a new era. You now have new information that will change the trajectory of your decision-making process and impact your life for the better. Feel into your genius, intuitive self. This is the space where great decisions are birthed. This is where your body knows how to heal. I am sure you can appreciate this awesomeness you already possess.

Now let's flip it over. If you are trying to make a decision, and you are in a negative headspace, maybe beating yourself up and not feeling good enough or worthy enough, wouldn't you agree that this negative mindset does not lend itself to achieving an outcome that will bring you joy, happiness, and success? In fact, your outcome is just the opposite. Has this ever happened to you? Have you ever made a decision when you were feeling badly and in a bad headspace? You probably made a not-so-great decision and got a not-so-great outcome. It's just how things line up.

No matter what's going on in your life right now, you have the genius inside of you. You are reading this book, which means you are a true genius. You are a genius resource finder. You already know how to find resources to support you in decision-making and tap into your own power. Even if that support is just me, you have the know-how right in front of you. I am going to show you each step. You have the guts, and you will soon have the clarity. You start here with "G", **G**enius. You are truly a genius decision-maker whose power has been hidden for too long.

For a little extra practice, use any technique you have up your sleeve to start from a positive mindset about your own genius. Come visit me over on social to get some more ideas, tips, and Go Power action on reclaiming your own Genius. You are a genius, you got this. You are capable of making great decisions. You will soon have the tools, the method, and the support as you practice becoming unstoppable at making decisions quickly, and with ease, because you are truly a genius at it! Know and feel your personal genius self.

ORDER OF OPERATION

It's time to grab your "GO" in using your "Go Power". Let's move on to step 2. "**O**" is for **O**perational. Let's look at the start of the simple seven. **G**enius **O**perational **POWER**. Ya, you got that.

Would you agree that it is easy to make decisions when there is a clear path to follow? A step by step order removes the guessing so you can feel confident about the plan. Right? First, do this, then do that, then voila, here's your answer. We talked about there being a clear process and procedure to follow in the medical, wellness, and even the real estate investing worlds. This allows for duplicatability of the process. It also allows for the ability to measure progress along each step. And if you miss a step, you'll know it because this affects the answer or the outcome. If A+B = C, and you skip adding the "B", you no longer know nor can predict the answer or outcome. There is a clear process to all development of nature, human biology, physiology, and the evolution of the world. There is an order of operation in all great mathematical equations, processes, best practices, and methodologies. So why wouldn't you apply an operational order to make your best decisions for yourself?

Honestly, you probably never placed an operational order in your decision-making because you did not know it existed, am I right? I never knew there was an order to follow with making decisions until very recently. But it makes sense. Of course, there is an order! Just like there is an order to your day, there is an order to decision-making. As you continue to move through these simple seven steps, you'll see why it makes sense to take action in the order that it is presented in your Go Power. Would you agree that it makes sense to use your **G**enius **O**perational **POWER** when making decisions? Heck to the YES! Of course, it makes sense. At least it will, once you have the operational order. But just the fact that you said, "Yes, I agree," signifies that you have said yes to yourself to follow the order of operation to support you in your personal genius decision-making. Don't forget you ARE the genius! And I agree with you. There should be a simple order of operation to make smart decisions for ourselves.

POWER IN YOUR PRESENCE

So far, this is super simple as promised, but hang tight, we are just getting to the good stuff. Grab your **G**enius **O**perational **POWER** and let's head over to step 3. The "**P**" in **P**OWER stands for being **P**resent. Be present before you make your decision. This is such an overused concept lately. Be present. What does this mean? Be awake? Be clear? Be active? Be mindful?

Well, according to Healthline.com, to be present means, "...you're focused and engaged in the here and now, not distracted or mentally absent." (Link). So why would being focused in the here and now help you make a better decision? As you can imagine, if you are the opposite of present and not focused on right now, then you are consumed with distracted thoughts and even distracted actions that are likely not helping you in making your best decision.

Be honest. Are you typically distracted when trying to make decisions? Are there too many people in the room? Do you have the pressure of time or lack of time? Distracted by the feeling of a lack of support? Lack of resources? Are you distracted by the uncertainty of the outcome even when you make a decision?

You may feel overwhelmed, angry, desperate, burdened, anxious, or even scared. These low-vibration emotions do not fuel the decision-making process in a productive way. I know that I've made many decisions in my past from this space of fear, anger, and despair. And I'm sad to report that the results of decisions made from this negative headspace were not productive results. The outcome was rarely as I wanted it, and the actions that followed became murky and often dead ends and did not net me what I desired.

Being present includes being aware of how you are feeling. I used to be really good at stuffing my emotions, so I didn't have to feel the gut-wrenching pain of negative emotions in my body. Of course, that backfired on me. I became an expert at keeping my emotions contained. Ignoring my emotions and making decisions from this non-present place. Unfortunately, I learned the hard way that this does not lead to a happily ever after story. Instead of feeling connected to my true power through presence, I then also had to deal with my negative emotions resurfacing as back pain, neck and shoulder tightness, stomach aches, and other ways my genius body was screaming at me to pay attention to the emotions I was hiding. Distracted by my body aches and pains continued the cycle of lack of presence when making important life decisions for myself and those impacted around me. I will share this chapter of my life another time, but for now, just know it was not a happy chapter.

So, how can you break the distraction cycle? How can you move from a negative headspace of distraction when making a decision to being present? The ultimate answer is that it takes practice to know when you are present and when you are not. And you also need to know what it feels like to actually be present and focused in the moment. If you are feeling eager, optimistic, or excited, these are good signs that you are indeed being more present and aware in the decision. Lower-vibration emotions such as depression, sadness, fear, revenge, and anger are a guide that you are not being present and are more focused on someone or something else instead of yourself.

Here are a few quick actions to help you become present in just a few minutes. Please keep in mind, it gets easier the more you practice these techniques, hence, practicing the art of presence is a real thing.

Fast Actions that foster personal presence:

- Five counts of deep breathing (see below for the exercise)
- A quick walk outside in nature
- Lie down on the earth
- Play in your garden
- Watch the birds
- Pet a dog or cat
- Laugh, sing, dance
- Go for a run or bike ride.

- Hop in the shower (people tend to find they are most present in the shower).
- Listen to your favorite happy song

Of course, there is also the well-known, meditation or simply being still. The list can go on and on. I would love to show you how to do any of these activities, ones that will open your ability to be present. For now, let's just use breathing as an example.

Sit in a chair with your tush not quite against the back of the seat with feet underneath you flat on the ground. Place your arms at your side or in your lap with palms facing up for openness or down for grounding. Either is fine. Try to sit up tall with your spinal vertebrae stacked versus slouching, as this helps open your central nervous system to being present. Take a breath in and a relaxing exhale breath out. Feel your body. Use pillows behind your back and/or under your arms or elbows to be more comfortable. Close your eyes. Breathe in through your nose for the count of three, then breathe out of your mouth for the count of six. Notice, you are breathing out twice as long as breathing in.

For those of you who like to understand the "why" behind an action, this is explained through physiology. Science studies show you how an oxygenated brain functions at a higher level. Have you ever seen those trendy oxygen bars? I've never used them myself, but they were derived from the concept that an oxygenated body is a higher-functioning, more present body. This fresh oxygen replenishes the cells throughout your body, resulting in feeling more awake, alert, and alive.

Unfortunately, most of us tend to hold onto carbon dioxide in our bodies. Carbon dioxide is a byproduct of oxygen or already-used oxygen. It is "A colorless, odorless gas. It is a waste product made by the body. Carbon dioxide travels in the blood from the body's tissues to the lungs." (Link) It serves an important role, and then we hold it in our lower lungs, some more than others, which takes up space, therefore, fresh oxygen coming in has no place to go. Breathing out longer than in allows time and more force to move CO_2 (carbon dioxide) out of the lower air sacs and out of your body through your breath. Your lungs now have space to bring fresh oxygen in to be utilized by your body.

Fueling your cells with fresh oxygen molecules is an easy and fast way to awaken your body to the present moment. I've used this technique with clients for years with great success. Clients tell me they can actually feel their body's power after this breathing exercise. I've even used it with people deeply suffering from breathing dysfunction who had decided to stop walking because of difficulty breathing. (*Disclaimer: Always consult your physician or a medical professional before adding or changing your exercise routines.) After working together, these clients achieved huge milestones of breathing easier than they had in years, walking further, having more energy, feeling stronger, expressing more calmness, and an overall better quality of life. They simply added this daily breathing technique practice which enhanced the power of presence.

In case you missed it, here it is again. Close your eyes. Breathe in your nose for the count of three, then breathe out of your mouth for the count of six. Repeat this process five times. It should take you about 60 seconds to complete. When you are done, open your eyes. Simply notice how you see things around you a little bit differently. Objects in the room are more vibrant or clear, your breathing will certainly be slowed and calmer. Your body will feel more relaxed. You have oxygenated your body and your brain with the goal of being present. You will be more open to listening for answers that come. These are the answers you've been waiting for. The answers that align with peaceful and maybe even joyful outcomes. When you have peace in your body, more peaceful decision-making occurs. When you feel peace in your body, this is your genius body telling you that what you are thinking is good and helpful to you. It is an indicator that what you are doing is beneficial, and will be more conducive to making decisions in alignment with bringing continued peace and happiness into your world. Have fun with this. Be playful about it. There is nothing serious going on here. Being present supports you in your goal of making decisions that are great for you!

KNOW YOUR OUTCOME

Now it's time to move onto step 4 of your GO POWER decision-making method. It's the "**O**" in your P**O**WER and represents the **O**utcome. This is where you get to step into acknowledging your desired outcomes during your decision-making process. This step in your **G**enius **O**perational **POWER** is exciting and truly important. You can not move towards your desired goal if you have not yet acknowledged what that desired outcome could be for you.

Always start with the end in mind. This helps to create a clearer path forward in the simple seven during your decision-making. Your outcome could be a big hairy audacious longer-term goal, or this could be your short-term, in view, desired outcome. When we connect again, we will spend more time on how to determine the short- and long-term outcomes, but for the sake of this lesson, let's pick an outcome that you want from a decision you're having to make right now.

Let's follow the Go Power decision-making method. You've stepped into your **G**enius knowing. You are following the **O**perational decision-making order. You did some quick breathing to be in a more **P**resent state. And now, you are ready to explore possible **O**utcomes you'd like to achieve from this decision. Let's pick a shorter-term or short-view outcome that you want. Maybe it's something you could achieve today, in the next few days, or next few weeks. It's okay and even highly recommended to dream big for those bigger decisions and bigger outcomes, but for today's practice, let's stick with a short-view, desired outcome. Does this outcome you want to achieve feel good when you're looking at it right now? If the answer is yes, then go ahead and write it down.

EXPLORE YOUR REASON WHY

This brings us to step 5 in harnessing your Go Power. The "**W**" in your PO**W**ER. "**W**" stands for your "**W**hy". Here we get to learn more about WHY this outcome is important to you. I know. I told you we would take the emotion out of making the best decision for ourselves, and I promise we will! The more you practice using your Go Power to make decisions, the faster you'll get at understanding what feels good and the real reason why you want the outcome you are seeking.

We don't have time for a deep dive into your #1 reason why you want your goal or outcome to be achieved, but let's use an example to understand how to locate your "why" behind your desired outcome.

Grab a scrap piece of paper and answer the following questions:

- Why is this outcome important to you?
- What will this outcome net you?
- Why is this new answer important to you?
- What will be different when you achieve this goal?
- How do you want to feel about achieving the outcome you indicated?

Can you see where this is headed? If you have written a page about why, or even just a paragraph, let's try to get this down to summarize your why in one sentence. One sentence that will sum up why this outcome is so important to you. Could you sum it up in one word? If not a single word, maybe a phrase. Something short enough that you will remember it, or you can write on a sticky note.

If you had a little relief in your belly while thinking about your reason why, or perhaps even a little tear bubbled up because it truly hit your soft spot, then you likely hit it right. This could very well be the reason why you want to achieve the outcome you indicated. Doesn't clarity feel great?!

EXECUTE YOUR PLAN

It's time to execute a plan! Grab your Go POWER, and let's explore "**E**", **E**xecute. Now, before you get too excited to start taking action, you have a bit of work to do in order to take the best action for you! You now know where you want to go and why you want to get there, but where are you now? Where are you starting from in this very moment? You can not create your map, until you know where you are starting from, agreed? This is the 'start' circle on your Go Power Map. You've already found the location of the treasure at the end, also known as your outcome. It makes sense that you also need to locate your starting point.

You may have an easy time recognizing where you are now. Some of you may be in denial. Others may be plain pissed off that you are not where you want to be, and here you stand in this place right now. Okay, yes, this may bring up some new emotions you don't want to deal with right now, but remember, you are so close to taking steps towards your outcome, so now is not the time to put any energy into beating yourself up. (Well, truth be told, I don't ever recommend beating yourself up.) Simply acknowledge that you are where you are and you are about to move forward.

We've all made mistakes that we are not proud of. We all have made decisions that did not go well or did not turn out as planned. So, let yourself off the hook. You've done your best given the situation or conditions, and now it's time to grow and move forward. Did you give yourself a hard, honest look in the mirror? Take a minute to write down where you are now, so we can get ready to execute your next step towards your desired outcome. Don't get lost in the weeds here. Look at where you are now. Look at where you want to land with this topic, and you already identified why it's important to you, which should help you stay focused. You are so close to feeling your true Go Power!

Now, choose a realistic next step(s). You may only have one step before your desired outcome, or there may be many steps in between. Maybe you need to collect some more information or do some research before knowing your next steps. That's okay, too. Can you see how using your Go Power can help you dial in on where you're headed and what your next steps are? There's more we could dig into here, but it's time to move on to your "R" in using your Go Power.

REVIEW, REVISE, RINSE, REPEAT

The R in your Go POWER is your rudder. The "R" stands for "Review" It's where you take a minute to review, revise, rinse, and maybe even repeat if that action step is truly bringing you closer to your desired outcome. You may be able to do this immediately, or your Review may come tomorrow, the next day, or later next week, depending on when it is appropriate to review your progress. This is a critical step in knowing if you are headed towards your outcome or away from your desired goal. The "R" in your GO POWER tells you if you are steering in the right direction on your map. If you review and see that yes, the action step has brought you towards your outcome, great! So now, what's the next step? Look again at where you are now, where you are headed, and why you want to achieve that desired outcome. Now pick the next action step. You are making smart decisions, making progress towards desired outcomes, and you will achieve your goals! Review, Revise, Rinse, Repeat. Review, Revise, Rinse, Repeat. You are doing it!

Use your GO POWER in all decision-making, big or small. Remember, you are a genius! There is a clear operational method. Be present, choose your outcome, and why you want this outcome, execute, and review. Now, simply Rinse and Repeat. With practice, you got this! Use your Genius Operational Power. Use your GO POWER to make good decisions in your life from here on forward. I'm in your corner. Let's connect. Send me a note through any of my social channels or website. I'd love to hear how using your GO POWER has supported you in making better decisions in your life.

Again, muscle memory does not occur from reading one single chapter once. To get a deep dive and build positive habitual patterns, jump on over to www.MeganWaiteCoching.com where we can stay connected and you can get more comfortable with using your new Go Power method regularly.

To You and Your GO Power,
Coach Meg

Megan Henry

Actor, Speaker & Author

https://www.linkedin.com/in/megan-henry-a8913725/
https://www.facebook.com/megan.henry.961/
https://www.instagram.com/officialmeganhenry/
https://meganhenryspeaks.com/home
https://vimeo.com/user4303366

Megan is a multifaceted actor, author, and producer who co-produced an award-winning socially-conscious short film with a diverse team to challenge the status quo and personal biases. By embracing diverse perspectives, the project fosters collaboration that leads to deeper understanding and more effective solutions for everyone involved. As a featured author in the bestselling book 1 Habit: How to Survive in a Post-COVID World, she emphasizes the importance of embracing both the mess and magic of life, encouraging readers to stay connected to their personal power amid life's paradoxes. Megan also empowers creative visionaries, storytellers, community leaders, to be the example of meaningful change they want in the world, by taking responsibility for their personal narratives—especially those shaped by trauma. Her work reminds us to cultivate inner stability to feel safe to express authentically and thrive with the diversity of life, without demanding acceptance or validation from others.

Celebrate Contrast – Using Conflict for Positive Transformation

By Megan Henry

1: Introduction to the Idea of Celebrating Contrast

Imagine a world where we celebrate contrast—a world where differences are an invitation to collaborate, expand conversations, and find solutions, not sources of division. I believe in this world. It's a world where we courageously welcome the potency of conflict as a gateway to cultural transformation and individual growth. Too often, we shy away from discomfort or disagreement, seeing it as a threat to be managed, avoided, or even eliminated. But what if these uncomfortable moments, these clashing perspectives, are precisely where we can discover our most transformative growth?

In today's social landscape, it's easy to view our differences as a reason for canceling or rejecting each other. Yet there is a profound opportunity in these moments of discomfort—a chance to expand our understanding, to reflect on why we're triggered, and to invite curiosity rather than resistance. Now, as you read this, take a moment to check in with your body. Notice what's coming up. Are you feeling resistance? Curiosity? Perhaps a belief you hold is being nudged, or something within you wants to be acknowledged. I invite you to let whatever is arising simply be, without judgment. In this space of acceptance, we allow contrast to teach us.

2: Early Struggles with Differences

My relationship with contrast and differences began early in life, though I didn't realize its significance at the time. I was adopted, and this reality challenged the norms of what a family was "supposed" to look like.

Growing up, I often felt the shadow of misunderstanding looming over me, and with it, the persistent question: "Where do I belong?" My existence felt unconventional, and while I've come to see myself as someone who challenges the status quo, this wasn't a natural or easy path. Instead, it often felt like a burden.

Whenever the subject of adoption surfaced, I was quick to shut it down. There was a painful sting in feeling like my family dynamic—a source of love and identity for me—was something others scrutinized or couldn't quite grasp. Rather than celebrating the unique story that brought me here, I found myself hiding it, fearful of judgment and discomfort. I longed to fit in, to feel that sense of "normalcy" that others took for granted. It felt safer to keep quiet, to avoid the hurt that came from being different. In those moments, I didn't recognize that my unique perspective was a gift, or that sharing it could enrich not only my life but the lives of those around me.

In time, I began to understand that by withholding my voice, I was not only diminishing my own experiences but robbing others of a fuller, richer understanding of what family, belonging, and identity could mean. The fear of judgment or rejection blinded me to the wisdom that lay in my story. I was canceling my own truth because it felt safer, but in doing so, I also canceled the opportunity for others to learn from my journey and for me to find healing in owning it. This was the beginning of my journey toward recognizing the value of embracing the discomfort of difference.

3: Understanding Triggers as Tools for Growth

As I moved through life and experienced more, I started to see how often I encountered people, beliefs, or perspectives that triggered something within me. Instead of viewing these moments as invitations to grow, I often felt threatened, retreating inward or judging the other person's perspective to protect myself. Over time, I've come to understand that these triggers are powerful mirrors—they reflect the places where I haven't yet found freedom from old beliefs or unresolved experiences. As Peter Crone, a teacher I deeply respect, often says, "Our triggers reveal where we aren't yet free." These moments, uncomfortable as they are, point directly to areas of our lives where healing and transformation are possible.

I realized that, instead of reacting defensively to these situations, I could choose curiosity. I could view my triggers as tools for self-discovery rather than threats to my identity. Embracing this mindset was revolutionary. I began to ask: "Why is this challenging for me? What does it bring up?" Each trigger became a doorway, a chance to explore and, ultimately, release energies I had been holding onto for years.

The same is true for how we relate to others in society. When we encounter differences that seem to challenge our values, our reflex might be to judge or dismiss them. But if we can pause and consider these perspectives without fear, they might reveal hidden layers of truth we hadn't previously considered. Triggers, then, aren't just nuisances— they're invitations to growth, if we are willing to do the work of transforming them.

4: A Story of Creative Conflict – The Film Collaboration

A few years ago, I had the opportunity to collaborate on a socially conscious short film with a friend who held a different view from mine. Initially, I was excited by the potential to create something meaningful that could disrupt the status quo and spark dialogue. But as I learned more about the project, I realized that my friend's narrative vision was grounded in perspectives that I didn't agree with. Suddenly, I was caught between my desire to use art to inspire change and my resistance to the story's direction.

My initial reaction was one of discomfort and rejection. I felt myself shut down, unwilling to support what felt like a perpetuation of popular yet, to me, limited narratives. I wanted to tell stories that embraced the full spectrum of our shared human experience—stories that inspired unity, love, and healing. But here I was, facing a collaboration that felt at odds with my values. My mind raced with reasons to walk away, to dismiss the project entirely, yet something deeper inside me felt expansive, urging me to stay. This was more than an artistic disagreement; it was a trigger pointing to unresolved fears and judgments within myself.

I had a choice: I could either close myself off from the project and my friend's perspective or approach it with curiosity. Why did his vision feel so uncomfortable for me? What beliefs was I clinging to that made me feel I couldn't participate? This was an opportunity, I realized, not only to expand the conversation through our collaboration but to expand my own perspective.

My intuition told me there was something valuable here—a chance to explore my own biases and grow beyond them. Instead of advocating my viewpoint, I allowed myself to inquire: "What is the intention behind his story? What might I learn from seeing this narrative through his eyes?" This shift allowed me to find common ground in a space that initially felt divisive. By surrendering my resistance and opening to the experience, I realized that we were both seeking to create meaningful dialogue, even if our approaches differed.

5: Breaking Free from a Fear-Based Mentality

From an early age, society teaches us to outsource our power. We're conditioned to believe that life is an "outside-in" game—where happiness, security, and self-worth rely on getting the right things, winning approval, or bending others to fit our comfort zone. This mentality creates a division between "us" and "them," where one group's success implies another's failure, perpetuating a scarcity mindset. It's a cycle of separation consciousness, one that roots us in fear, division, and an endless loop of comparison and hierarchy.

But recent discoveries by scientists and physicists reveal a new way to see the world. Many now suggest that our universe may be holographic, with everything we observe in the external world reflecting our internal state—both individually and collectively. We live in a physical dimension governed by contrast, duality, and polarity, not as obstacles, but as essential tools for growth and understanding. Carl Jung once said, "The greater the tension, the greater is the potential." This tension, however uncomfortable, serves as a crucible for transformation and self-discovery.

If we genuinely want to live freely, compassionately, and expansively, we must take responsibility for our own narratives. Are they rooted in fear or love? When we see the world solely through the lens of fear, we grasp only fragments of truth—our "small truths." But fear can only take us so far. If we wait for others to change first or demand that our surroundings conform to our comfort level, we end up only scratching the surface of real transformation. We remain trapped in ego, mistaking our limited perspective for the entirety of reality, blind to a larger, more unifying truth.

6: Recognizing the Power of Contrast and Diverse Perspectives

In this journey, I came to a profound awareness: our unique perspectives, especially those that stand in contrast to each other, are elements of expansion. Each difference, rather than threatening unity, adds to the richness of our collective human experience. Diverse perspectives have the power to inspire grander conversations and innovative solutions. It's not about asserting who is right and who is wrong, but about leaning into the alchemy that comes from respecting and understanding opposing views. Through this lens, contrast becomes a powerful catalyst for healing, unity, and growth.

Yet, we give so much power to fear. We've been conditioned to shun, cancel, or criticize ourselves and others simply because we fear that diverse ideas might disrupt our comfort. By doing this, we inadvertently play small, withholding our unique perspectives in the hope that we'll be loved, accepted, or approved by others. We end up shrinking from the authentic expression of our truth, holding ourselves back from making the impact we're here to create. In our attempt to avoid rejection or judgment, we often cancel ourselves first—long before anyone else has the chance to.

But true love isn't conditional. And, quite frankly, sometimes the boat needs to be rocked.

When we approach our discomfort with ruthless compassion, we move beyond fear into understanding. Instead of viewing the perspectives of others as threats, we can view them as invitations to witness our own unconscious beliefs. In every trigger, there's a story waiting to be uncovered and healed. By celebrating our differences with curiosity rather than condemnation, we make room for deeper compassion and understanding, both for ourselves and others. After all, we didn't come here to simply "get along"; we came to activate the highest potential of our souls, and contrast is the sacred catalyst in that process.

7: Bridging the Great Divide – From Division to Discovery

So, how do we bridge this divide between divisiveness and discovery? How do we cultivate a mindset where uncomfortable conversations reveal hidden treasures rather than deepen our divides?

Here are three practical steps that I've found transformative:

1. Feel the Discomfort and Lean into Contrast

When we encounter perspectives that challenge us, it's natural to feel discomfort, often as a physical sensation in our bodies. Where it feels safe to do so, lean into this feeling and allow it to broaden your perspective on yourself and others. Take a moment to ask: "What is this discomfort trying to teach me?"

2. Observe with Compassionate Curiosity

Become a compassionate witness of your own experience. Approach yourself with gentle curiosity, acknowledging what surfaces without judgment. By getting into your heart and body, you can observe what the trigger is inviting you to discover. Rather than advocating rigidly for one "truth," let inquiry guide you. This mindset allows you to bridge divides, creating a more unified, richer experience of life.

3. Stop Waiting for External Permission

Instead of waiting for others to grant you permission, pivot your focus to the inner wisdom of your intuition. Let your inspiration and insights guide you rather than seeking validation or approval from institutions or conventional thinking. Trust the transformative power of your unique perspective to expand the conversation. Be willing to reach across the aisle as an observer, open to the wisdom in differences, rather than as a judge who needs to be "right."

8: A Call to Collaborate in Contrast

Our differences are opportunities to explore who we truly are, to challenge limiting beliefs, and to grow. When we feel an impulse to cancel or reject, we are often invited to find greater compassion for ourselves and others. By embracing this mindset, we can come together inspired by our differences rather than in spite of them.

Are you ready to disrupt divisiveness and engage with the transformative power of diverse perspectives? Are you willing to step into the expansive potential of collaborating in contrast? If you feel inspired to join in this movement toward unity, I'd love to hear from you. Together, let's cultivate a world that is enriched by our differences, where we lean into the contrast and grow.

JOIN THE MOVEMENT!
#BAUW

Becoming An Unstoppable Woman
With She Rises Studios

She Rises Studios was founded by Hanna Olivas and Adriana Luna Carlos, the mother-daughter duo, in mid-2020 as they saw a need to help empower women worldwide. They are the podcast hosts of the *She Rises Studios Podcast* and Amazon best-selling authors and motivational speakers who travel the world. Hanna and Adriana are the movement creators of #BAUW - Becoming An Unstoppable Woman: The movement has been created to universally impact women of all ages, at whatever stage of life, to overcome insecurities, and adversities, and develop an unstoppable mindset. She Rises Studios educates, celebrates, and empowers women globally.

Looking to Join Us in our Next Anthology or Publish YOUR Own?

She Rises Studios Publishing offers full-service publishing, marketing, book tour, and campaign services. For more information, contact info@sherisesstudios.com

We are always looking for women who want to share their stories and expertise and feature their businesses on our podcasts, in our books, and in our magazines.

SEE WHAT WE DO

OUR PODCAST

OUR BOOKS

OUR SERVICES

Be featured in the Becoming An Unstoppable Woman magazine, published in 13 countries and sold in all major retailers. Get the visibility you need to LEVEL UP in your business!

Have your own TV show streamed across major platforms like Roku TV, Amazon Fire Stick, Apple TV and more!

Learn to leverage your expertise. Build your online presence and grow your audience with FENIX TV.
https://fenixtv.sherisesstudios.com/

Visit www.SheRisesStudios.com to see how YOU can join the #BAUW movement and help your community to achieve the UNSTOPPABLE mindset.

Have you checked out the *She Rises Studios Podcast?*

Find us on all MAJOR platforms: Spotify, IHeartRadio, Apple Podcasts, Google Podcasts, etc.

Looking to become a sponsor or build a partnership?

Email us at info@sherisesstudios.com

www.ingramcontent.com/pod-product-compliance
Lightning Source LLC
Chambersburg PA
CBHW061704120626
46550CB00003B/1082